HANDMADE PICKLES & PRESERVES

HANDMADE PICKLES & PRESERVES

TRADITIONAL ACCOMPANIMENTS
FOR MEAT, CHEESE OR FISH

'To a past generation, the art of preserving and pickling was quite familiar, but in the great rush to the towns, old traditions were lost ...To restore the knowledge may be one way to make a happy and contented people, for there is more in it than reducing the cost of living; there is a satisfaction which comes from creative and productive occupation, and the culture of self-reliance which is the backbone of freedom.'

Herbert Mace, *Storing, Preserving & Pickling*, 1940

Contents

Introduction

'Simple, well-made preserves are most valuable domestic stores, as they will retain through the entire year or longer, their peculiarly grateful and agreeable flavour, and supply many wholesome and refreshing varieties of diet through the winter months and spring.'

Eliza Acton, *Modern Cooking for Private Families*, 1845

It's the little things in life that make a big difference.

My earliest food memories are of a kitchen, the pervading smell of boiling vinegar, with a pan on the stove containing anything from real tomato chutney to Pontack catsup. These were always consumed with great enthusiasm – some might even say with relish! Writing this book has made me remember the unending desire I had as a small boy to taste, smell and touch everything. I recall walks with my father, each one an adventure, when we gathered some booty from the side of the path to chew on, or more likely to take home. There he would transform it, like a wizard, into concoctions to excite the palate and engage the mind. These occasions formed my views of preserving, in particular the creation of the savoury sauces that are such an integral part of our daily lives without us ever really noticing them. That's what a 'tracklement' – a savoury jelly or sauce – should be: never dominating, always an adjunct to a meal or a dish.

I'm not sure how or why British food ever picked up its reputation for being bland and uninteresting; my experience is that we are a nation full of flavours and spice, and keen on exploration, heading out to the four corners and returning with sauces and techniques that have become embedded in our food culture. For example, since our company, Tracklements, started in 1970, my father and I have collected 400 or so books on food preservation, its traditions and place in our history.

According to my family, my great-grandmother would sit at the end of the table and cry, 'Pass the tracklements!' It was her belief that no particular meal was complete until the accompanying condiments had been placed, put or spread onto whatever was in front of her. I agree with that sentiment. Life is always a little less colourful without a perfectly balanced pickle on a piece of pork pie, or the pleasurable chomp of chutney in a sandwich filled with your favourite cheese or meat.

There is something reassuring about sharing food that our parents and grandparents loved with the next generation. In doing so, we regain and return to our foodie and cultural roots. Savoury preserving is all about that; every family has a favourite heirloom chutney or pickle made by a relative and treasured through the generations.

The home preserver begins a process of the enjoyment and sharing of food. We hope that this book will send you out on your own adventure and give you the confidence to embark on a wonderful journey: a journey that will enable you to make your own collection of tracklements to enhance your food and delight your friends. It is about discovery and a bit of detail. As you will see from the following recipes, we have always been a nation of adopters and adapters – more usually out of necessity coupled with invention. But some hard-and-fast rules must be observed, after which the budding preserver can add his or her own flourish and embellishments.

Don't be tempted to cut corners or to break the essential preserver's rules, but do experiment with levels of spicing. We think that these are the key part of the tracklement-maker's art. They add the light and shade to almost all the recipes in this book. Where we have specified an amount of fruit or vegetables to an amount of sugar and vinegar, it's important to follow that guidance. If you prefer something a little sharper, add a bit more vinegar – but make sure you compensate by removing an equal amount of sugar.

Welcome to the world of *Tracklements*. The aim of this book is to share with you the tricks of the trade that we have learned over the years and to encourage you to join in our culinary adventuring. We hope it will become a faithful friend and ally in the kitchen.

Guy Tullberg of Tracklements

Preserving essentials

There are few things as satisfying as popping open a jar of a homemade preserve and breathing in the scent of the luxurious flavour within. As only an aroma can, it will immediately transport you to the moment of harvesting the fruit, or watching the pot bubbling away on your cooker.

The diversity of preserves, from a mature chutney to a fresh relish, is matched only by the variety of the foods with which they can be eaten, but whether they are sweet or sharp, hot or fruity, smooth or chunky, they share a common goal: to bring out the best in whatever they are served alongside and to add a burst of flavour.

We call these recipes 'savoury', although it is hard to confine them in this way. They are so versatile, so adaptable; there is barely a meal or a dish that wouldn't benefit from the addition of one of them.

To make these jewels of your larder requires some essential elements which we have outlined below:

1. Acetic acid

This comes either in the form of lemon juice or vinegar. While lemon juice is straightforward acetic acid, vinegar is alcohol that has been exposed to air and turned into acetic acid. This acid prevents bacteria from growing in pickles and preserves, enabling them to keep their flavour and integrity for months or even years after they have been made.

There are many, many types of vinegar. Generally the variety originates from the national drink of the country it comes from. France, Spain and Italy and other wine-producing countries or regions produce red or white wine vinegar or vinegars from specific wines such as champagne or sherry, Italy produces its famous balsamic vinegar, England produces malt vinegar and cider vinegar (our favourite), and Scotland produces spirit vinegar – distilled malt vinegar which is useful in pickling as it is clear.

Vinegar used for pickling must have an acetic acid content of at least five per cent. We usually recommend using a really good-quality cider vinegar because of its sharp taste and fruity flavour. Wine vinegar contains sulphites, which is why we avoid using it. Some of the recipes use malt vinegar for its stronger flavour; it has an attractive darker colour and tends to have a slightly higher acetic content. We also use spirit vinegar on the rare occasions that we require high acidity but little or no flavour.

2. Sugar

Sugar is key in preserving, not only because flavour is captured by cooking with sugar, but also because it is important for achieving a good shelf life as well as getting a set in jellies and fruit cheeses.

The recipes in this book use either raw cane sugar or muscovado sugar. The 'raw' of 'raw cane sugar' refers to the fact that this sugar is unrefined. It is pale gold in colour with a hint of molasses. Muscovado sugar is also an unrefined cane sugar, usually much darker in colour and moist with a deeper, more treacly taste. We recommend using unrefined or raw sugars because they contain the minerals and nutrients that are stripped out during the refining process. Moreover, they are not exposed to the chemicals used in refining white and brown sugar, so while refined sugars contain practically no nutritional value, raw cane sugar contains phosphorus, calcium, iron, magnesium and potassium – all good stuff.

3. Spices

Essential in preserving, these are used to enhance flavour, making the end product richer or warmer and adding depth and dimension. They may amount to the smallest percentage in your preserve, but they give it its character. Fresh spices are best; ground ones will keep their flavour for up to six months, while whole ones will keep their's for a year.

We suggest using spices in a number of different ways; some products benefit from using the whole spice, some from using ground spice. There are products for which we suggest using a spice bag and removing the spices before bottling, which will keep the level of spicing constant. Other products that have the spices left in them will mature, develop and change flavour over time. There are further recipes where the vinegar is spiced before being used to create a gentler, different spice profile. We always recommend using whole spices when making mustard in order to retain all their essential oils. These are the most frequently used spices in preserving:

- **Allspice** A native of Jamaica, these largish red-brown berries are so-called because their flavour resembles a mixture of cloves, black pepper, nutmeg and cinnamon.
- **Chillies** Fresh chillies range from warm to super-hot, depending on their ranking on the Scoville scale. Our reaction to chilli is as unique to us as our fingerprints, but the Scoville scale is a measure of how much capsaicin is contained in a chilli, and therefore how hot it is. Jalapeño chillies, for example, score between 3,500 and 8,500 on the Scoville scale, whereas habanero and Scotch bonnet chillies score between 100,000 and 350,000. We always recommend using fresh chillies; in this way you avoid the 'chilli burn', and although the heat may be

fierce and intense, it will fade away more quickly and completely than if a chilli powder is used. Be careful when handling fresh chillies; wear thin rubber gloves if need be and avoid contact with your eyes. Green chillies are milder than their red counterparts. As with sundried tomatoes, drying chillies concentrates the flavour, which makes them hotter per gram than fresh chillies. The drying process cannot give them more heat than they started with, but concentrates it in a lighter weight ingredient. If a dried chilli were to be rehydrated, it would be as hot as a comparable fresh chilli.

- **Cinnamon** Cinnamon is the dried bark of a Sri Lankan tree and is sold as 'quills', which are long sticks of rolled bark. It has a beautifully sweet, warming taste that is used in both sweet and savoury cooking.

- **Cloves** These dried flower pods are painful and unpleasant to crunch on, so they should always be removed from the preserve prior to bottling. They have a tremendously strong sweet flavour, so are used sparingly. They also have an anaesthetic effect – so much so that for many years clove oil was used as a treatment for toothache.

- **Coriander seeds** These small, round, pale brown seeds are aromatic and oily and are very popular for flavouring Indian curries.

- **Cumin seeds** Made up of tiny, light-brown seeds, cumin is used extensively in Indian and Asian cooking.
- **Fresh ginger** Originally from Southeast Asia, this knobbly root has always played an important part in flavouring Indian and Asian food. It has a strong, peppery, sweet flavour and should be peeled prior to use. Its skin will wrinkle with age, so look for pieces of root with smooth skin.
- **Ground ginger** Fresh ginger and dried ginger differ dramatically in their flavouring effects. In ground ginger the oils and juices present in the fresh root have been removed. They are therefore used in different preserves to create different flavour profiles.
- **Nutmeg** Nutmeg is a hard, dusty-brown seed, whose fleshy red covering is dried and used as mace, another spice. Nutmeg has a gentle, aromatic warmth and a delicate nutty flavour.
- **Peppercorns** Peppercorns, black, white and green, are the whole dried berries of a tropical vine. They have a strong, aromatic flavour and have been highly prized as a seasoning since antiquity. Black peppercorns are the most pungent. White peppercorns are fully ripe berries with their outer skins removed. Green peppercorns are simply the unripe berries which are usually sold in brine to keep them soft and stop them from drying out. Ground pepper loses its aroma and flavour quickly so always use freshly ground as and when required.
- **Tamarind** This is the dark-brown pulp from inside the pod of the tamarind tree. It is characterised by its unique sour, acid flavour.
- **Turmeric** Fresh turmeric is a little root. Usually used in its ground form when it is bright yellow. It has a distinctive and warming taste.

4. Salt

Salt is used in pickling primarily to draw the liquid out of the vegetables or fruit in order to inhibit bacteria and prevent spoilage. It is also used for seasoning because it enhances the flavour of the preserve. We use only sea salt because of its purity; some table salts contain anti-caking agents that can cloud brines and distort flavours.

5. Time

The importance of time cannot be overstated. Time is required at the preparation stage, the cooking stage and (perhaps most challengingly) at the waiting-to-eat stage. Allowing preserves time in the jar before opening gives the flavours a further opportunity to infuse, evolve, mature and meld together to give a deeper, richer taste. Preserves cannot be hurried, but your patience will be rewarded because time will give your preserves sophistication and a complexity of flavour that will make your labours all the more gratifying.

Preserving rules

Making preserves is simple if you follow a few rules, so relax, have fun, experiment and put your own personality into your preserves.

- As with all food, you cannot make a silk purse from a sow's ear. The quality of what comes out is dependent on the quality of what went in. Only the very best ingredients will create the very best end result.
- In order to achieve the desired shelf life, the correct balance of sugar and vinegar to solids is essential. However, if you prefer your preserve a bit sharper and less sweet, the vinegar content can be increased by the same amount as the sugar content is decreased. This may result in a slightly 'looser' preserve.
- The fruit or vegetables should be perfect, without bruises or blemishes. Ripe or just under-ripe is best, particularly for jelly-making. Don't be tempted to use over-ripe fruit or vegetables as they might ferment in the jar. Equipment should be spotlessly clean to prevent any bacteria from getting into your preserves.
- The sugar should never be added too early in the cooking process as it essentially stops the fruit or vegetables from cooking and will make any skins go hard.
- Once you have filled your jars, leave them to cool for 24 hours or so. The jars cool down more quickly if they are not touching one another. Jars become hot once they are filled with the hot preserve, so the less you touch them while they cool down, the better. This is most important when making jellies in order to maintain clarity.
- Store in a cool, dry place.
- Most preserves will keep for a year or more if packed and stored correctly. As a rule, relishes, with their shorter cooking time, will keep for up to six months.
- There is inevitably a lot of fruit and vegetable preparation and chopping involved when making preserves and this takes time. As cooking times can be key and boiling mixes don't generally wait, it's best to do all the chopping, dicing, peeling and crushing before you start cooking – which is why we have detailed what to do with the fruit or vegetables in the ingredients list in most of the recipes.
- Once opened, jellies do not need to be stored in the fridge. They will just take up space unnecessarily and will go hard and crystalline (this is also true of onion marmalade).

Tools of the trade

The chances are that you already have everything you need to make preserves in your kitchen, but it's worth checking and getting all the equipment together before you start the recipe. As a general guideline, make sure you have:

A large pan

A preserving pan or large, heavy-bottomed saucepan is a must. Big is best; it needs to be able to hold all the ingredients without boiling over, and should be wide enough to allow for rapid evaporation of liquid, which is why many preserving pans are wider at the top than at the bottom. The heavy base helps to spread heat evenly and prevents the preserve from catching and burning. For making pickles, chutneys and any other preserve that uses vinegar, a stainless-steel pan is best. Copper is not suitable as the vinegar corrodes it and it will spoil both the colour and flavour of your preserve.

Kitchen scales

You need a really accurate set of scales. Preferably choose one that can weigh accurately right down to 1g–2g in weight, as spices are light and using the right amount is important. However, in order to make things easier, we have, wherever possible, put spice amounts in teaspoons and tablespoons as well as their metric measures. Always use level spoonfuls.

Muslin or a jelly bag

This is used for straining juice from the fruit pulp in jelly-making; muslin can also be used to make a spice bag (see left). At Tracklements we use two layers of muslin in a large sieve set over a measuring jug or bowl. You can also upturn a stool and sling the muslin from the legs to make a homemade jelly bag, but fruit pulp and juice is very heavy so take care to attach the corners securely. It is recommended that you submerge the jelly bag or muslin in boiling water for a couple of seconds before using: this is called scalding and it helps the juices run through the bag rather than being absorbed into it.

Jars and bottles

Glass is perfect, not only because you can see your beautiful handiwork but also because it is non-corrosive. These days most jar lids are plastic-lined but do check that the lids aren't made of anything that might corrode. Old

To make
a spice bag

Take a piece of muslin approximately 10cm (4 inches) square, put the spices in the middle and gather up the outside edges. Tie up with a piece of string so that the spices are held securely in the pouch. You can also use the string handle to tie the bag to the side of your preserving pan to keep the spices immersed in the liquid.

coffee jars are not suitable, as they don't form an airtight seal. Small, straight-sided jars are perfect for turning fruit cheeses out onto the cheeseboard.

Keep large jars for preserves you think will be devoured most quickly, as preserves deteriorate more quickly once the jar has been opened and they are exposed to the air. Wide-necked jars best suit chunkier preserves and tall bottles are best for marinades and dressings.

Jars and bottles all need to be perfectly clean. Any bacteria must be killed off or it may contaminate the preserve and make it inedible. If you are reusing jars, the easiest way to ensure they are sterilised is to run them through a hot wash in a dishwasher; failing that you can sterilise clean jars by half filling them with water and putting them in a microwave (without their lids), heating on full power until the water has boiled for at least a minute, then carefully swirling the water around the jar before pouring away.

Alternatively, use the oven method: stand the jars on a baking tray lined with baking paper with their lids resting on the top of the jars. Turn the oven on and heat to 110°C/225°F/Gas ¼ and bake for 30 minutes. Leave to cool slightly before filling.

Bowls

Plastic, ceramic or glass bowls of varying sizes are indispensable for brining, mixing and collecting juice. Metal bowls are best avoided in case they affect the taste of the preserve.

Sieve, colander and slotted spoon

Nylon, plastic or stainless-steel sieves and colanders are needed for straining juice in jelly-making and for pressing fruit through in ketchup-making. We also recommend using a little sieve (approximately 10cm/4 inches in diameter) for skimming scum off the surface of jellies. You can also do this with a large slotted spoon.

Funnel and a small plastic jug

A plastic funnel or a small plastic jug means that you don't have to have an incredibly steady hand when bottling hot ketchups. However you fill your jars, they are bound to get sticky on the outside – it is one of the unwritten laws of preserve-making! You may find it easy to spoon your mixture into the jar, or to use a ladle, but we recommend using a funnel or a small plastic jug to dip into the mixture in the pan, then pour into the jars. A quick wipe of the outside of the jars with a damp cloth while they're still warm will clean up any stickiness.

Jar sizes

Where a recipe says 'Makes x jars/bottles', we've worked on the basis of a 'normal' jar being 350g (12oz), a small one 200g (7oz) and a bottle 350ml (12fl oz or 1½ cups).

A mouli or food mill

This is great fun to use when making a fruit purée for ketchups and cheeses, as it removes stones, pips and much of the skins, but is not essential. Some moulis come with a selection of fine, medium or coarse discs. A spatula or the back of a wooden spoon and a sieve will work just as well, but can be much harder work.

Utensils

- **A large wooden spoon with a long handle** Wood is best because it is a bad conductor of heat and therefore won't take any heat out of the mixture, thereby affecting the boil. A wooden spoon won't scratch your pan or burn your hand, either.
- **A sharp knife** Chopping, slicing and dicing are necessary and fundamental stages of preserve-making, so a good, comfortable knife for these tasks is indispensable.
- **A peeler** Fruit and vegetable skins can be off-putting in a chutney, so the ingredients usually need to be peeled first.
- **A spatula** Because nothing should be left on the sides of the pan!

A mini food processor, stick blender or nut and seed grinder

This is really useful if you want to save on chopping, pulping and grinding, especially small amounts of garlic, herbs or mustard seeds.

A pestle and mortar

An essential piece of kit for crushing and grinding small amounts of seeds and spices.

Labels

Not only are they important in making your jars look beautiful, but it's helpful to know what preserve you have put in which jar when you come to open them many months later. Wait until the jars are cold before adding the labels.

Kitchen skills

How to remove seeds from a chilli

The chemical that gives chillies their heat – capsaicin – is not, as is widely believed, contained in the seeds but in the placenta, which is what the seeds are attached to. Removing the seeds is optional, although doing so will ensure the placenta is also removed and means your preserve won't have lots of seeds in it. Halve the chilli lengthways with a small, sharp knife. Scrape out the seeds and cut away the white ribs from each half. Wash your hands well after touching chillies and avoid contact with your eyes.

How to chop an onion

Onions release a gas when cut, which reacts with the water in our eyes to form a mild but irritating sulphuric acid. Our eyes react by trying to flush the irritant away; the result is that chopping onions can leave us red-eyed and tearful. A way to combat this is to put the onions in the fridge for half an hour before chopping them; this slows the chemical reactions within the onion. But it also helps if you can minimise the time spent chopping, and therefore a sharp knife and an efficient method of chopping them will really help. Peel the onion, leaving the root end on. Cut the onion in half and lay one half, cut-side down, on a board. Make two horizontal cuts towards, but not through, the root and several vertical cuts lengthways towards the root. Then slice the onion across working towards the root into diced pieces.

How to crush garlic without a garlic press

Peel cloves by putting a large-bladed knife flat on the clove and pressing it down with the heel of your hand; this flattens the clove a little and means the skin will simply drop off. Then chop the garlic finely, sprinkle it with a little salt, put the knife blade at a 45° angle and press down really firmly, scraping it across the garlic, squashing the chopped bits under the knife and along the board. Repeat this action until you have a paste.

How to grind whole seeds

For large quantities, use a blender, food processor or retired coffee grinder, but for small amounts use a pestle and mortar. Using the pestle to pound the seeds is one way to open them, but may result in seeds flying all over your kitchen. Another way is to bring the pestle down on the seeds, then pull it towards you across the bottom of the mortar, thereby grinding the seeds to a finer grind.

PICKLES

'Pickles, etc., apart from possessing considerable food value,
make a tasteless meal appetizing, stimulate the appetite and
relieve the monotony of an otherwise dull meal.'
Cyril Grange, *The Complete Book of
Home Food Preservation*, 1947

Pickling is where preserving all began. The original (and for a long time, only)
method of storing the glut of the seasons, pickling is the forefather of preserving,
from which all modern chutneys and relishes are descended. What started from
necessity has developed into a much-loved food embellishment – the food flourish
on the plate! The culinary aim of pickling is to make something truly delicious,
with a good crunch and bite that invigorates the palate and livens up the meal. The
scientific aim of pickling is to create an environment where the natural bacteria that
cause vegetables to decay cannot live.

What a relief it must have been for our ancestors to find a way of storing the
flavours of summer safely for enjoyment during the barren winter months, especially
in countries where the growing season was short. Methods of pickling vary according
to the civilisations in which they started. The Romans, for example, relied on verjuice
(sour grape juice) or vinegar to keep vegetables edible, whereas in Asia the salted
juice of fermented fish and soybeans was used, and this became the base for many
of the sauces and ketchups we enjoy today. Irrespective of their provenance, what all
pickles had in common was their importance to the various cultures that benefited
from them, and their legacies echo in the food customs and traditions of many
modern eating habits.

One of the earliest references to pickling is in the 1st-century writings of a
Roman soldier and farmer called Lucius Junius Moderatus Columella, who wrote
De Re Rustica, a treatise on agriculture, in which he says, 'Vinegar and hard brine
are essential for pickle-making.' He goes on to detail his methods for pickling most
things, from olives to turnips. Robert May, author of the mighty 17th-century tome

The Accomplisht Cook, and his contemporary John Evelyn were early exponents of the pickler's art. They pickled vegetables, fruit and even nasturtium flowers, which were used for garnish, and they both wrote widely on the subject. However, the golden age of British pickling didn't begin until the middle of the 19th century when sugar and spices became increasingly available to the domestic cook. Eliza Acton and Mrs Rundell were just two of those who took full advantage of the influx of sugar and spice. In their writings you can see the domestic cook's enthusiasm for preserving absolutely everything. Nothing was to be wasted.

From a simple desire to preserve what could be grown at home, pickling evolved into an adoption and incorporation of flavours that had been tasted abroad and brought home by returning explorers and adventurers. The British have always been as inquisitive and exploratory in their culinary adventures as in their travelling ones.

Today, there are two distinct types of pickling: one that involves preserving whole vegetables such as onions, called clear pickles; and the other, which mainly concerns us here, that combines mixed vegetables in a sauce, called sweet pickles.

Making pickles

The key to making a beautifully crisp and bright pickle is speed and freshness. The key to enjoying it is to let it mellow in the jar for over a month. By and large, pickles accompany cold food: a hand-raised pork pie or a ploughman's can be elevated from snack to feast by a good pickle.

There are generally only five ingredients needed to make a marvellous pickle: vegetables, salt, vinegar, sugar and spices. Pickles nearly always feature vegetables rather than fruit, and in order to meet the culinary aim of pickle-making we must obey the first rule of pickling, which is that the vegetables must be fresh.

In order to satisfy the scientific aim, a salt or brine is needed. The vegetables are chopped and left in a salt-and-water brine, or they are dry-salted for up to 24 hours. Dry-salting gives a crunchier pickle, but both methods, by a simple process of osmosis, draw the liquid from the vegetables and remove the possibility of spoilage. As a rule of thumb, a wet brine should be 10 parts water to 1 part salt.

Although salting and brining are both cheap, easy and reliable ways of preserving vegetables, various old cookery books mention that the brine should be tested when made to ensure that it is strong enough to float an egg in. This stems from the historical vagaries in the quality of salt, and isn't necessary nowadays as we are fortunate enough to be able to rely on modern salt's strength to do the job; it's also a bit chancy as it doesn't account for the age of the egg! If you're making your own brine, we recommend that you use a good sea salt, as table salt sometimes contains additives that may discolour the brine.

After salting or brining, pickles are stored in an acid environment (vinegar), which further inhibits the development of bacteria. We use a very good-quality cider vinegar and recommend you do too, as vinegar plays an important part in the end taste, and cider vinegar has a beautifully gentle flavour that has the added benefit of tasting of apples. You can, of course, use any vinegar you choose, as long as it has an acetic content of at least five per cent, but cider vinegar is natural, contains nothing scary and there are some very good producers.

When a pickle recipe calls for the mixture to be boiled, it generally only needs to be brought up to the boil very briefly – just long enough so that it can be filled into jars while it is hot to aid preservation and draw a vacuum.

Piccalilli

Piccalilli is one of the first pickles that was widely adopted. An all-time favourite and essential if you live in the land of pork pies, ham or Cheddar cheese, this fiery, creamy, mustardy piccalilli will serve you well no matter what the British weather may do to your summer picnic plans. Make it at the end of one summer to enjoy the next.

Piccalilli should contain a variety of crunchy vegetables in a smooth mustard sauce. The vegetable choice is up to you, but we've opted for a traditional selection. Unless you grow your own, small pickling onions are hard to find, so choose the easy option and go for a jar of pickled silverskin onions instead.

Makes 4–6 jars

700g (1lb 9oz) mixed vegetables, cut into 1cm (½-inch) cubes; we like to use:
500g (1lb 2oz) cauliflower
50g (1¾oz) or ½ red pepper
50g (1¾oz) or ½ green pepper
100g (3½oz or 1 cup) green beans – French or young runner beans – topped and tailed

1 litre (1¾ pints or 4 cups) brine (100g/3½oz or scant ½ cup sea salt dissolved into 1 litre/ 1¾ pints/4 cups water)

250g (9oz or about 2 cups) pickled silverskin onions, drained and diced

250g (9oz or 2 cups) gherkins, drained and diced

20g (¾oz or 2 tbsp) cornflour

3 tsp ground turmeric

730ml (25fl oz or 3¼ cups) cider vinegar

170g (6oz or scant 1 cup) raw cane sugar

4 tbsp mustard powder

100g (3½oz) strong English mustard

1. Put the mixed vegetables in a bowl, pour over the brine so that they are completely covered, cover and leave for 24 hours. Drain and rinse well to remove the excess brine.

2. Mix the onions and gherkins into the vegetables.

3. Mix the cornflour and turmeric with 25ml (1 tablespoon + 2 teaspoons) of the vinegar and stir to make a smooth paste. Put the remaining vinegar, the sugar, mustard powder and strong mustard into a heavy-bottomed pan and heat gently, stirring, until the sugar has dissolved. Slowly add the cornflour paste, stirring well, then bring to the boil.

4. Lower the heat and simmer for 5 minutes until the mixture is just thicker than a good double cream.

5. Add the vegetable mixture to the pan and bring to the boil, stirring gently. Remove from the heat and carefully spoon the mixture into sterilised jars. You will need to press the mixture down in the jar to ensure the vegetables are covered by the sauce. Seal immediately.

Bengal pickle

We first started making this sweet-and-sour pickle thanks to our local organic farmer. He told us about the difficulties he was having in getting supermarkets to buy his organic carrots because they were wonky and ugly. That was enough to get us rummaging through our cookbook library to find out what we could do with them. We unearthed a Sophie Grigson recipe, and after a few trials, tests and alterations we made this beautiful pickle. It's the perfect thing for piling onto poppadoms.

Makes 4–6 jars

5 carrots, finely grated

2 fresh red chillies, deseeded and finely chopped

1 tsp coriander seeds

25g (1oz or approximately 1½ tbsp) sea salt

750ml (26fl oz or 3¼ cups) cider vinegar

380g (13oz) or 2 Bramley apples, peeled, cored and finely chopped

5 cloves of garlic, peeled and finely chopped

25g (1oz) fresh ginger root, peeled and finely chopped

750g (1lb 10oz or 3¾ cups) raw cane sugar

1. Place the carrots, chillies and coriander seeds in a large bowl and stir well. Mix in the salt and cover with 550ml (19fl oz or about 2½ cups) cider vinegar. Cover the bowl with a wet cloth and leave overnight.

2. The next day, put the remaining 200ml (7fl oz or scant 1 cup) vinegar and the apples into a large, heavy-bottomed preserving pan and bring to the boil. Lower the heat and simmer until the apples are completely soft and pulpy.

3. Add the carrot mixture to the pan. Add the garlic and ginger, and bring to the boil.

4. Once the mixture is boiling, add the sugar and stir well. Bring back to the boil, stirring all the time, until the mixture is thick and jam-like. Take off the heat and put straight into sterilised jars. Seal immediately.

Hot aubergine pickle

Aubergines, being native to India where they are prized for their versatility, are the vegetable of choice when making a hot, authentic Indian pickle. This is a classic example of a brinjal pickle: fiery and highly spiced with a delightful fresh taste. Guy fell in love with aubergine pickle at an Indian restaurant in London where the food was intensely hot but the heat didn't burn, nor did it linger. We think it's the perfect accompaniment to a lamb curry.

Makes 4–6 jars

1kg (2lb 4oz) or 2–3 aubergines, cut into 5-mm (¼-inch) cubes

50g (1¾oz or 3 tbsp) sea salt

400ml (14fl oz or 1¾ cups) cider vinegar

2 large onions, peeled and finely chopped

3–4 fresh red chillies, deseeded and finely chopped

20g (¾oz or 2 tbsp) sultanas, roughly chopped

150g (5½oz or 1 generous cup) tomato purée, concentrated

1 tsp tamarind paste

150g (5½oz or ¾ cup) raw cane sugar

150g (5½oz or ¾ cup) dark muscovado sugar

For the curry paste

generous ½ tsp) fenugreek seeds

1½ tsp coriander seeds

1 heaped tsp cumin seeds

generous ½ tsp yellow mustard seeds

1½ tsp cardamom pods

1 tsp black peppercorns

1. Sprinkle the aubergines with the salt and mix to make sure the salt covers all the pieces. Transfer to a colander. Place a plate, slightly smaller than the diameter of the colander, on top of the aubergines with a weight on it. Put the colander on a draining board or in a bowl so that any water that is expelled doesn't go everywhere. Leave for 4 hours.

2. While the aubergines are doing their thing, make up the curry paste by putting the fenugreek, coriander, cumin and mustard seeds, and cardamom pods and peppercorns into a small bowl or mug with 2 tablespoons of vinegar. Leave to soak for 1 hour, then whizz in a food processor or use a stick blender to create a paste.

3. Put the remaining vinegar into a large, heavy-bottomed preserving pan, add the finely chopped onions and boil for 5 minutes until the onions are soft. Add the chillies, sultanas, tomato purée, tamarind paste and curry paste and bring back to the boil. Add the sugars and stir until completely dissolved. Bring back to the boil and add the aubergines.

4. Simmer for 5–10 minutes, or until the desired consistency is achieved – it should be quite thick. Remove from the heat, then spoon the pickle immediately into sterilised jars. Seal immediately.

Farmhouse pickle

Firm believers in the simple pleasures of life, whenever we have lunchtime visitors to Tracklements, we always serve cold ham, cheese, faggots, pork pie and locally made organic bread. We think it's a feast fit for every hungry soul and perfect for trying an assortment of tracklements. But however much we like variety, this farmhouse pickle is something we can't help coming back to time and again. With 14 ingredients it nearly tops the chart, but despite the length of the list, it's simple and easy to make.

Makes 4–6 jars

1kg (2lb 4oz) mixed vegetables, cut into 5-mm (¼-inch) cubes; we like to use:
2 medium carrots
2 medium courgettes
3 medium parsnips
1 turnip
1 medium onion, peeled

40g (1½oz or 2 heaped tbsp) sea salt

530ml (19fl oz or approximately 2½ cups) malt vinegar

15ml (½fl oz or 1 tbsp) lemon juice

½ fresh red chilli, deseeded and finely chopped

1 heaped tsp ground allspice

500g (1lb 2oz or 2½ cups) muscovado sugar

75g (2¾oz or generous ½ cup) dried dates, chopped

15g (½oz or approximately 1 tbsp) tamarind paste

225g (8oz or 1 cup) tomato purée, concentrated

1. Mix the prepared vegetables together in a bowl and add the salt, stirring well to ensure that they are well covered.

2. Transfer the vegetables to a colander. Place a plate, slightly smaller than the diameter of the colander, on top of the vegetables with a weight on top. Put the colander on a draining board or in a bowl so that any water that is drawn out of the vegetables can drain off. Leave for 24 hours.

3. Drain the vegetables and rinse well to remove any excess brine.

4. Heat the vinegar and lemon juice in a preserving pan. When they start to simmer, add the vegetables. Bring to a gentle boil, then add the chilli and allspice, stirring well.

5. Add the sugar in stages, stirring well to make sure it's dissolved, and bring back to the boil.

6. Add the dates and tamarind paste and boil for approximately 5–10 minutes, or until the desired consistency is achieved, then stir in the tomato purée giving the mixture a final stir. Take off the heat and put straight into sterilised jars. Seal immediately.

Bread & butter pickle

Bread and butter pickles were originally made from anything left over in the kitchen garden at the end of the summer. This is a fresh, vibrant pickle that admirably demonstrates how satisfying, fulfilling and rewarding the simple things in life can be. Slather it on a hunk of fresh bread and butter, or top a burger with it, put your feet up and enjoy. The taste of this pickle conjures images of haystacks, bright-blue skies, swallows diving and looping and the feel of warm summer grass under bare feet.

Makes 4–6 jars

3 large cucumbers, diced

800g (1lb 12oz or 3½ cups) red pepper, deseeded and finely diced

800g (1lb 12oz or 3½ cups) green pepper, deseeded and finely diced

2 medium onions, peeled and finely chopped

90g (3¼oz or scant ⅓ cup) sea salt

400ml (14fl oz or 1¾ cups) malt vinegar

650g (1lb 7oz or 3¼ cups) raw cane sugar

1 fresh red chilli, deseeded and finely chopped

45g (1½oz or 4 tbsp) yellow mustard seeds

20g (¾oz or 2 tbsp) cornflour, mixed with a little water

1. Put the cucumber, peppers and onion into a colander and sprinkle with the salt, then stir well. Place a plate, slightly smaller than the diameter of the colander, on top of the vegetables with a weight on top. Put the colander on a draining board or in a bowl so that any water that is drawn out of the vegetables can drain off. Leave for 24 hours.

2. Heat the vinegar in a large, heavy-bottomed preserving pan. Add the sugar, chilli and mustard seeds. Bring to the boil and stir so that all the sugar dissolves. Add the diced vegetables and bring back to the boil. Simmer for 5–10 minutes, stirring occasionally. Add the cornflour paste and enough water to thicken and when it has reached a good consistency take off the heat.

3. Put the hot pickle straight into sterilised jars. Seal immediately.

Lemon pickle

With the rise of the East India Company in the early 19th century, the number of British aristocracy travelling in India increased dramatically – as did the popularity of Indian-influenced pickles. Lemon pickle was a direct attempt to copy those exotic flavours. This version is taken from a recipe written by Mrs Rundell in her 1842 book catchily entitled *A New System of Domestic Cookery Formed upon Principles of Economy and Adapted to the Use of Private Families by a Lady*. Both tangy and hot, the pickle is delicious with cold chicken.

Makes 5–7 jars

1kg (2lb 4oz) unwaxed lemons

60g (2¼oz or 3 heaped tbsp) sea salt

40g (1½oz) fresh ginger root, peeled

5 cloves of garlic, peeled

3–4 fresh red chillies, deseeded

10g (¼oz) fresh horseradish root

300ml (10fl oz or 1½ cups) cider vinegar

450g (1lb or 3 cups) sultanas

700g (1lb 9oz or approximately 3½ cups) raw cane sugar

20g (¾oz or 2 tbsp) yellow mustard seeds

1. Chop the lemons, skins and all, into eighths, then put in a bowl, sprinkle over the salt and mix well so that the salt is well distributed. Cover and leave for 24 hours. Don't rinse the lemons before you add them to the pickle as the salt left on them will counterbalance their acidity.

2. The next day, put the ginger, garlic and chillies in a food processor or blitz them with a stick blender for a couple of seconds until they are all very finely chopped. Then transfer to a bowl and set aside. Peel the horseradish and put it and 50ml (2fl oz or scant ¼ cup) of the cider vinegar into the food processor. Whizz until the horseradish is finely chopped, then add the sultanas and give another quick whizz just to chop them slightly.

3. Put the remaining 250ml (9fl oz or 1 cup + 2 tablespoons) cider vinegar in a preserving pan with the sugar and heat, stirring constantly, until all the sugar has completely dissolved. Bring to the boil, then add the lemons with the ginger mixture and mustard seeds. Boil briskly for 5–10 minutes, then add the horseradish mixture, stir and remove from the heat. Spoon into sterilised jars while still hot. Seal immediately.

Courgette pickle

Courgettes seem to be ready to harvest all at the same time. No matter how hard the gardener tries to space them out, there will always be a glut and you can only eat so much ratatouille! This pickle is a wonderful way to capture the essence of summer and enjoy your crop throughout the year.

Makes 6–8 jars

5 medium courgettes, sliced into 5-mm (¼-inch) rounds

2 small onions, peeled and finely chopped

2 red peppers, deseeded and diced

60g (2¼oz or 3 heaped tbsp) sea salt

300ml (10fl oz or 1¼ cups) cider vinegar

1 tsp ground turmeric

generous ½ tsp ground nutmeg

1 tsp celery seeds

½ tsp fresh red chilli, deseeded and finely chopped

1 tsp yellow mustard seeds

280g (10oz or about 1½ cups) raw cane sugar

1. Mix the courgettes, onions and red pepper in a bowl. Sprinkle in the sea salt and mix thoroughly so that all the vegetables are coated.

2. Transfer to a colander and place a plate, slightly smaller than the diameter of the colander, on top of the vegetables with a weight on it. Put the colander on a draining board or in a bowl so that as the water is expelled it doesn't go everywhere. Leave for 12 hours.

3. Drain the vegetables and rinse thoroughly to wash off any residual salt. Pat dry with kitchen towel or a dry tea towel.

4. Put the vinegar, spices, celery seeds, chilli and mustard seeds into a large, heavy-bottomed pan and heat. Add the sugar and stir until completely dissolved. Bring to the boil and add the vegetables. Lower the heat and simmer for 5–10 minutes, then remove from the heat and spoon into sterilised jars. Seal immediately.

Hot garlic pickle

We were given this recipe by the runner-up at a chutney-making competition who called it 'The Kind Colonel's Chutney'. The story goes that the young subalterns of a regiment based in India found the local food, and in particular the local pickles favoured by the 'Old Brigade', too fiery-hot for their tastes. The lucky ones had a colonel whose sympathetic wife took pity on them and encouraged the cooks to produce something they would find more palatable. Still powerfully hot, this is a wonderfully aromatic and fresh pickle.

Makes 5–7 jars

650g (1lb 7oz) or about 20–25 heads garlic, divided into cloves and peeled

50g (1¾oz or 3 tbsp) sea salt

5g (⅛oz) fresh bird's-eye chillies

10g (¼oz) or approximately 60 dried bird's-eye chillies

500g (1lb 2oz) fresh ginger root, peeled

500ml (18fl oz or 2¼ cups) cider vinegar

500g (1lb 2oz or 3¼ cups) sultanas

160g (5½oz or 1 cup) currants

1.5kg (3lb 5oz) tomatoes, chopped

15g (½oz or 1 tbsp) sea salt

500g (1lb 2oz or 2½ cups) raw cane sugar

300g (10½oz or 2⅓ cups) tomato purée, concentrated

1. Start by dry-salting the whole, peeled garlic cloves. Put them in a bowl and sprinkle 35g (1¼oz or scant 2 tablespoons) of sea salt on top, mix well, then cover with a weighted plate and leave for 4 hours. Then give the cloves a good rinse to get rid of any excess salt, then chop into quarters.

2. Put the fresh chillies, dried chillies and ginger in a food processor and give them a good blitz so that there aren't any large pieces. Pour in the vinegar, add the sultanas and currants and whizz together for 10 seconds.

3. Put the tomatoes in a large, heavy-bottomed pan with the chopped garlic, remaining salt and the contents of the food processor. Bring to the boil. Add the sugar and stir until it has completely dissolved, then bring back to the boil.

4. Boil for 10–15 minutes, stirring frequently. Add the tomato purée, bring back to the boil, then immediately remove from the heat and spoon into sterilised jars. Seal immediately.

Beetroot pickle

Beetroot is the sweetest vegetable in the kitchen garden. It has a
mellow, earthy taste and a vibrant colour that it is apt to share too
generously with your hands when making this preserve. Perfect for
cold meats, this pickle has a delightfully gentle crunch.

Makes 6–8 jars

1kg (2lb 4oz) beetroot – leave
on the skins and at least
2.5cm (1 inch) of stalk

1 litre (1¾ pints or 4 cups) brine
(100g/3½oz or scant ½ cup sea
salt dissolved into 1 litre/
1¾ pints/4 cups water)

750ml (26fl oz or 3⅓ cups)
cider vinegar

700g (1lb 9oz) or approximately 5
Bramley apples, peeled, cored
and finely chopped

800g (1lb 12oz or 4 cups)
raw cane sugar

2 medium onions, peeled and
finely chopped

15ml (½fl oz or 1 tbsp)
lemon juice

1 tsp sea salt

25g (1oz or approximately
3 tbsp) cornflour mixed with
25ml (1 tbsp + 2 tsp) water

1. Blanch the beetroot by bringing a pan of water to the boil and adding
the whole beetroot to it, then bringing it back to the boil for 3–5 minutes,
depending on size. Take out and rinse under cold water to stop them
cooking. When cool enough to handle comfortably, peel the beetroot and
discard the skins. Using a sharp knife, top, tail and cut the beetroot into
1-cm (½-inch) cubes. Put the cubes into a bowl with the brine. Cover and
leave for 24 hours.

2. The next day, put the vinegar and apples into a large, heavy-bottomed
preserving pan, bring to the boil, lower the heat and simmer gently until
the apples are soft and pulpy.

3. Add the sugar and stir until it is completely dissolved. Bring back to
the boil and add the onions, lemon juice and salt, and simmer for a further
10 minutes.

4. Add the cornflour paste to the boiling mixture, stirring frequently until
it reaches the desired thickness – about 2 minutes.

5. Drain and rinse the beetroot to ensure no brine remains, then add it to
the pan and stir for 30 seconds before taking it off the heat. Spoon into
sterilised jars and seal immediately.

CHUTNEYS

'The composition of these favourite oriental sauces varies but little
except in the ingredient which forms the basis of each. The same
piquant or stimulating auxiliaries are intermingled with all of them
in greater or less proportion.'
Eliza Acton, *Modern Cookery for Private Families*, 1845

Homemade chutneys are the secret weapons of the larder, transforming simple
dishes into sumptuous feasts and adding a swell of intense flavour to everything they
accompany. They are the vivacious and big-hearted guests at the table, as at home on
the side of a plate of cold meats or cheese as they are adding depth to a stew. Surely
the most versatile of all our side-of-the-plate accompaniments, chutneys are as easily
paired with hot or cold food. An apricot or peach chutney with curry is every bit as
good as it is with cheese.

The word 'chutney' derives from the Hindustani word Caṭnī, variously translated
as 'to lick or taste', 'intensely spiced', or 'spiced relish'. In the past chutneys were
served alongside every meal in India, where they were used as a respite
for the diner from the heat of the curry. These accompaniments
wouldn't necessarily have been preserved but were most
often made fresh, to be eaten immediately.
They featured locally grown fruit
and vegetables with spices such
as turmeric, cumin, tamarind and
ginger, all of which were prized for
their medicinal qualities as well as
for their flavour. With the advent
of the fast tall ship, trade routes
to the East opened up, and India
became a major centre for global

trade. The British who worked and travelled there discovered a passion for the Indian chutneys, and in true explorer fashion started adopting another country's cuisine and adapting it to their taste. Consequently, the first Indian chutneys began to arrive back home, along with the spices that were required to make them. These luxury imports were mostly mango chutneys, and they formed the basis for British copies that originally appeared in cookbooks as 'mangoed' fruit or vegetables.

Dried fruits and spices remained expensively traded for several centuries and were therefore the preserve of the wealthy and highly prized as exotic ingredients. These ingredients were used as embellishments in chutneys to a greater or lesser degree, depending on the extent to which the cook wanted to show off.

Throughout Victorian times, as sugar and spices became more accessible, enthusiastic cooks continued to experiment with more and more ingredients. Mangoes gave way to home-grown fruit and veg. Apples and onions started to become the stars, and the spicing became milder and tailored to accompany more traditional British foods. Their popularity assured, chutneys began to appear commercially at the end of the 19th century, but as with a great deal of British food, the quality of these commercial offerings suffered during two world wars, and home pickling became, once again, a necessity.

Today, chutneys answer our basic love of great taste, thrift and creating something beautiful from scratch. We may not need rows and rows of them along larder shelves as the Victorians did; nonetheless, there is something wonderfully reassuring about spying a jar of chutney sitting on a shelf with its promise of summer harvests and sweet-and-sour fruitiness.

Making chutneys

The defining characteristics of good chutneys are their soft, chunky textures and the princely melding of flavours. By a simple combination of fruit, vegetables, spices, sugar and vinegar, we can create sophisticated and complex flavours, extraordinary in their versatility.

The most important rule, and really the only one to remember when making chutney, is that it is the combination of sugar and vinegar that preserves the fruit or vegetables in the chutney; therefore the overall quantity must not be altered, although the balance between them can be tweaked to allow for a sweeter or sharper end flavour.

As with other methods of preserving, one of the most important ingredients is time. The difference between a chutney and a pickle is that a chutney is cooked gently and slowly for a longer period. This concentrates the flavours of the ingredients and thickens the chutney by evaporating the liquid and concentrating the vinegar – which is why chutneys should never be covered during cooking. As the age-old adage says, the best things come to those who wait, and this is certainly true of chutneys. Time is not only key in the making, but as the flavours will continue to mature and intensify in the jar, it is best to keep your jars of fruity goodness for at least two months before eating, and more if patience allows.

While it is certainly true that it is really only worth preserving the best fruit and vegetables, it is also true that chutneys are invaluable for using up the gluts of the seasons and the fruit and vegetables that are left in the veggie plot at the end of the summer. That doesn't mean that the fruit or veg can be over-ripe or old, but it does mean there is a little leeway with under-ripe fruit, although bruised fruit should always be avoided.

Spices are vital. Without these tiny powerhouses, a chutney would be a flat, colourless canvas without the intriguing flavours that prod and poke around the tongue and make the final product so appealing. Because they are so important, it is always best to use really fresh spices. There are several ways to spice a chutney, depending on the end result you want to achieve. There are times when pre-ground ginger is preferable to using fresh for the taste it bestows on the end result; similarly, some chutneys benefit from having the spices left in the end product where they will carry on maturing and strengthening in flavour, some from using a spice bag that is removed after the cooking and others from using the spices only to flavour and infuse the vinegar. It all depends on the taste and piquancy you want to achieve; the longer the spices are simmered in the preparation, the stronger their flavour in the final chutney.

As you will see from the following recipes, we recommend cooking the fruit and vegetables first before adding the sugar. This is because the sugar essentially starts the preservation from the time it is added, and so halts the cooking of the rest of the ingredients. The type of sugar used will affect the end flavour; raw cane sugar gives a lovely light flavour and muscovado sugar endows the chutney with its treacly, heavy, molasses flavour.

At Tracklements, we only use cider vinegar, partly because of its purity but also because we love its flavour. Like wine vinegar it keeps the colour of the vegetables used, and if the recipe calls for a spiced vinegar it takes on the complexities of the spices beautifully.

As long as the balance of sugar and vinegar is enough to preserve the fruit or vegetables being used, there is no such thing as a chutney that doesn't work. The number that can be made is virtually limitless. It is true, however, that some flavours work blissfully well together and some scratch and niggle at each other; if you're unsure then start with the tried-and-tested recipe favourites that won't let you down.

A couple of final tips will help with the process of cooking your chutney. Towards the end, stir the chutney frequently to prevent it from catching on the bottom of the pan. The way to tell when your chutney is ready is to draw the spoon through the mixture along the base of the pan; if the channel created in the chutney takes a second or two to fill (rather than filling immediately), then your chutney has reached the right consistency. Always fill the sterilised jars when the chutney is hot and to within 5mm (¼ inch) of the top, and put the lids on quickly. That way the chutney will create a vacuum in the jar as it cools and the air in the neck of the jar contracts. This will help ensure that your labours will last for at least a year.

Rosie's rhubarb chutney

Rosie Brown won our 'make a chutney' competition in *Country Living* magazine with this delicate, fruity chutney. We made it, and the profits from its sale went to Farm Crisis Research, a charity nominated by Rosie.

Rhubarb, like courgettes, seems to be one of those plants that grow voraciously in any space; consequently kitchen gardeners frequently find themselves with rather more than they know what to do with. This chutney is the perfect solution.

Makes 4–6 jars

1kg (2lb 4oz) rhubarb, washed, trimmed and cut into 2-cm (¾-inch) chunks

2 lemons

25g (1oz) fresh ginger root, peeled

5 cloves of garlic, peeled and crushed

500g (1lb 2oz or 3½ cups) sultanas

500g (1lb 2oz or 2½ cups) raw cane sugar

500g (1lb 2oz or 2½ cups) muscovado sugar

½ tsp curry powder

½ tsp cayenne pepper

600ml (20fl oz or 2½ cups) cider vinegar

1. Put the rhubarb into a large, heavy-bottomed preserving pan over a low heat. Pare the skin from the lemons. Bruise the ginger, then put the lemon skins and ginger into a muslin bag and tie it to the side of the pan, low enough that it will be covered by the other ingredients.

2. Squeeze the juice from the lemons and pour it over the rhubarb, then add the garlic. Put the sultanas, sugars, curry powder and cayenne pepper in the pan, add the vinegar and give it a good stir.

3. Bring to the boil and stir continuously until the sugar has completely dissolved. Lower the heat and simmer gently for 45 minutes, stirring frequently to make sure the chutney doesn't catch on the base of the pan, until the desired consistency is reached. Test it by running a spoon along the bottom of the pan; if the channel you make doesn't fill immediately, the chutney is ready.

4. Remove the pan from the heat. Discard the muslin bag and spoon the chutney into sterilised jars. Seal immediately and store for two months before using.

Tomato & onion chutney

This was one of our first chutneys. It came about thanks to The National Trust, a longstanding customer, who asked for an authentic kitchen-garden chutney. At the time it was only the enthusiastic home cook who made good-quality chutneys like this, so we gleefully took up the challenge to create a chutney that would taste as good as homemade – without having to make it at home.

Makes 4–6 jars

350ml (12fl oz or 1½ cups) cider vinegar

3 medium carrots, peeled and cut into 1-cm (½-inch) chunks

2–3 large onions, peeled and diced

1 medium Bramley apple, peeled, cored and diced

600g (1lb 5oz) tomatoes, chopped

100g (3½oz or about ⅔ cup) dried dates, chopped

3 cloves of garlic, peeled and crushed

20g (¾oz or 4 tsp) sea salt

½ tsp freshly ground black pepper

1 tsp ground allspice

1 tsp ground ginger

1 fresh red chilli, deseeded and finely diced

330g (11½oz or 1⅔ cups) raw cane sugar

1. Put the vinegar and carrots in a large, heavy-bottomed preserving pan and bring to the boil. Lower the heat and simmer for 5 minutes.

2. Add the onions and continue simmering until both the onions and carrots are soft.

3. Add the apple, tomatoes, dates, garlic, salt, spices and chilli, stir and bring back to the boil. Boil for 5 minutes before adding the sugar, stirring continuously until the sugar is completely dissolved.

4. Boil for 30–40 minutes, or until the desired consistency is reached, stirring regularly to stop the chutney catching on the base of the pan. Test by running a spoon along the bottom of the pan – if the channel you make doesn't fill immediately, the chutney is ready.

5. Remove the pan from the heat, pour the chutney into sterilised jars, seal immediately and store for two months before using.

Rich tomato chutney

Because he wanted his children to eat something better than the ubiquitous 'Tommy K' with homemade burgers and chips, Guy set about making a chutney with a true, deep, vibrant tomato flavour – that satisfies the requirement of wholesomeness. This chutney is like an old friend, and will wrap its arms around you in a comforting hug.

Makes 3–5 jars

1kg (2lb 4oz) tomatoes

2 medium onions, peeled and diced

250ml (9fl oz or 1 cup + 2 tbsp) cider vinegar

3 cloves of garlic, peeled and crushed

½ fresh red chilli, deseeded and finely chopped

1 tsp sea salt

40g (1½oz or 2 tbsp) tomato purée, concentrated

50g (1¾oz or approximately ⅓ cup) sultanas

200g (7oz or 1 cup) raw cane sugar

1. To peel the tomatoes, use a sharp knife and make a cross incision in the skin on the bottom of the tomatoes. Then put them in a bowl and cover with boiling water for 1–2 minutes, or until their skins split and come off easily. Discard the skins. Cut the tomatoes into chunks.

2. Put the onions and vinegar in a large, heavy-bottomed preserving pan and bring to a gentle boil for 5 minutes to soften the onions.

3. Add the garlic, chilli and salt. Give a good stir, then add the tomatoes, tomato purée and sultanas and bring back to a rapid boil.

4. Add the sugar and stir well until all it has all dissolved.

5. Boil for 45 minutes–1 hour, or until the desired consistency is reached, stirring regularly to stop the chutney catching on the base of the pan. Test by running a spoon along the bottom of the pan – if the channel you make doesn't fill immediately, the chutney is ready.

6. Remove the pan from the heat, pour the chutney into sterilised jars and seal immediately. Store for two months before using.

Green bean chutney

When our Operations Director, Ben, told his family he was coming to work at Tracklements he was immediately presented with his mother-in-law's recipe for Green Bean Chutney. Like many chutney recipes, this one has been passed down from mother to daughter through time, with each generation gently adapting it to suit modern tastes, but like my grandfather's axe, it remains true to its origins. Crunchy in texture and pickle-like in character, it's a good alternative to piccalilli. Adding the beans at the end helps keep their squeaky crunch.

Makes 3–5 jars

500g (1lb 2oz or 3 heaped cups) green beans (French or bobby), topped and tailed and chopped into 2-cm (¾-inch) lengths

400ml (14fl oz or 1¾ cups) malt vinegar

2 medium onions, peeled and diced

100g (3½oz or ⅔ cup) sultanas

2 tsp fresh red chilli, deseeded and chopped

300g (10½oz or 1½ cups) raw cane sugar

2 tsp yellow mustard seeds

2½ tsp ground turmeric

1 tsp sea salt

20g (¾oz or 2 heaped tbsp) cornflour

1½ tbsp mustard powder

1. Blanch the beans by putting them into salted boiling water for 3 minutes, then drain and rinse with cold water to stop them from cooking further. Set aside to drain.

2. Put the vinegar, onions, sultanas and chilli in a large, heavy-bottomed preserving pan and boil for 5–10 minutes to soften the onions. Add the sugar, mustard seeds, turmeric and salt to the pan and stir.

3. Mix the cornflour and mustard powder with 1 tablespoon of water to make a paste and stir slowly into the pan. Boil for 5–10 minutes until the desired consistency is reached, stirring regularly to stop the chutney catching on the base of the pan. Test by running a spoon along the bottom of the pan – if the channel you make doesn't fill immediately, the chutney is ready.

4. Take the pan off the heat and add the green beans, then spoon the chutney carefully into sterilised jars and seal immediately. Store for two months before using.

Apricot & ginger chutney

We made this chutney over 20 years ago to accompany curry; pure and simple. It adheres closely to the precepts set out in those early British chutneys that emulated the Indian originals, using exotic dried apricots alongside the more readily available indigenous apple. The limits of its helpfulness in the kitchen and on the table are yet to be found and we think it is as delicious as it is versatile.

Makes 4–6 jars

600g (1lb 5oz or approximately 3½ cups) dried apricots, roughly chopped

Boiling water, enough to cover the apricots

400ml (14fl oz or 1¾ cups) cider vinegar

500g (1lb 2oz) or approximately 3 Bramley apples, peeled, cored and chopped into 1-cm (½-inch) pieces

2 cloves of garlic, peeled and chopped

30g (1oz) fresh ginger root, peeled and finely diced

30g (1oz or generous 1½ tbsp) sea salt

½ fresh red chilli, deseeded and very finely diced

600g (1lb 5oz or 3 cups) raw cane sugar

150g (5½oz or 1 cup) sultanas

1. Put the dried, chopped apricots into a heatproof bowl and just cover with boiling water. Leave for 30 minutes.

2. Tip the apricots and any remaining liquid into a large, heavy-bottomed preserving pan, add the vinegar and bring to the boil. Add the apples, garlic, ginger, salt and chilli, bring back to the boil, lower the heat and simmer for 10 minutes, or until the fruit has relaxed.

3. Add the sugar slowly while stirring continuously. When the sugar has completely dissolved, add the sultanas and boil for 20–30 minutes, or until the desired consistency is reached, stirring regularly to stop the chutney catching on the base of the pan. Test by running a spoon along the bottom of the pan – if the channel you make doesn't fill immediately, the chutney is ready.

4. Remove the pan from the heat, pour the chutney into sterilised jars and seal immediately with lids. Store for two months before using.

Spiced plum chutney

A wet spring followed by a warm, dry summer creates an abundance of stone fruit – which means that come the beginning of September, the fruit trees should be dripping in plums and damsons. We wanted to make a chutney that was slightly sharper than the usual so we used Stanley plums that are barely ripe, kept the vinegar content quite high and added orange zest and mustard seeds. The result was this gloriously tart, fruity chutney.

Makes 4–6 jars

600ml (20fl oz or 2½ cups) cider vinegar

2–3 medium onions, peeled and diced

1kg (2lb 4oz) plums, stones removed, roughly chopped

400g (14oz) or approximately 2 Bramley apples, peeled, cored and roughly chopped

350g (12oz or 1¾ cups) muscovado sugar

300g (10½oz or 1½ cups) raw cane sugar

4 cloves of garlic, peeled and finely chopped

30g (1oz) fresh ginger root, peeled and finely chopped

10g (¼oz or 2 tsp) sea salt

1 tsp grated orange zest

1 tsp yellow mustard seeds

1 tsp ground nutmeg

½ tsp ground cinnamon

½ tsp freshly ground black pepper

30g (1oz or about 2½ tbsp) sultanas

1. Heat the vinegar in a large, heavy-bottomed preserving pan. Add the onions. Bring to the boil, lower the heat and simmer for 5 minutes to soften the onions. Add the plums and apples and bring back to the boil. Cook for 10 minutes.

2. Add the sugars to the pan, stirring continuously until they are both completely dissolved. Bring the mixture back to the boil and add the garlic, ginger, salt, orange zest, mustard seeds, spices and sultanas. Stir well.

3. Continue boiling until the correct consistency is reached, stirring regularly to stop the chutney catching on the base of the pan. Test by running a spoon along the bottom of the pan – if the channel you make doesn't fill immediately, the chutney is ready.

4. Remove the pan from the heat, pour the chutney into sterilised jars and seal immediately. Store for two months before using.

Christmas chutney

Whenever we open a jar of this chutney at shows we always hear people exclaim, 'It tastes just like Christmas!' Laden with fragrant spices like allspice, nutmeg, cinnamon and ginger, it's best to let this chutney mature in the jar for two months or so for the full flavour to develop – which is why we make it in the autumn ready for eating with the cold cuts of meat on Boxing Day.

Makes 4–6 jars

300g (10½oz or 3 cups) fresh cranberries (if you can't find fresh, frozen will do)

350ml (12fl oz or 1½ cups) cider vinegar

2–3 medium onions, peeled and diced

750g (1lb 10oz) or 4–5 Bramley apples, peeled, cored and chopped into 1-cm (½-inch) chunks

80g (3oz or ½ cup) currants

400g (14oz or 2 cups) raw cane sugar

250g (9oz or 1¼ cups) muscovado sugar

35g (1¼oz or 2 tbsp) sea salt

4 cloves of garlic, peeled and crushed

1 small fresh red chilli, deseeded and finely chopped

½ tsp ground ginger

½ tsp ground nutmeg

½ tsp ground cinnamon

½ tsp ground allspice

1. Put the cranberries into a food processor and give them a quick blitz – or use a stick blender. The aim is to just chop them, not blitz them to a pulp. Set aside while you put the vinegar and onions in a large, heavy-bottomed preserving pan, bring to the boil, lower the heat and simmer for 5 minutes.

2. When the onions are soft add the apples and the cranberries and bring back to the boil for a further 5 minutes, stirring occasionally until the apples start to relax.

3. Add the currants and mix in, then add the sugars, salt, garlic, chilli and spices, stirring continuously until the sugars have completely dissolved.

4. Boil for 30–40 minutes, or until the desired consistency has been reached, stirring regularly to stop the chutney catching on the base of the pan. Test by running a spoon along the bottom of the pan – if the channel you make doesn't fill immediately, the chutney is ready.

5. Remove the pan from the heat, pour the chutney into sterilised jars and seal immediately. Store for two months before using.

Green tomato chutney

At one time every gardener would have had a recipe for this chutney, as green tomatoes were devilishly difficult to get to ripen at the end of the summer, so there were always leftover fruits that couldn't be eaten raw. What better way to deal with them than turn them into a deliciously rich, intensely flavoured chutney? We meet many people on our travels around the country who have family heirloom green tomato chutney recipes and have tried many variants. This one remains one of our all-time favourites.

Makes 3–5 jars

For the spice mix
½ tsp fenugreek seeds
½ tsp each coriander seeds, cumin seeds, black peppercorns and cardamom seeds
½ tsp brown mustard seeds

For the chutney
350g (12oz) or approximately 2 Bramley apples, peeled, cored and chopped into 1-cm (½-inch) chunks
200ml (7fl oz or scant 1 cup) cider vinegar
700g (1lb 9oz) green tomatoes, chopped into chunks
4 cloves of garlic, peeled and crushed
15g (½oz or 1 tbsp) sea salt
1 fresh red chilli, deseeded and chopped
425g (15oz or 2 cups + 2 tbsp) muscovado sugar
35g (1¼oz or approximately 2 tbsp) raw cane sugar
350g (12oz or 2 cups) dried seedless dates, roughly chopped

1. Preheat the oven to 200°C/400°F/gas mark 6.

2. Spread the spices thinly on a baking tray and roast in the oven for 4 minutes, shaking the tray once after 2 minutes. Allow the spices to cool for 10 minutes before lightly grinding them using a pestle and mortar. Set aside.

3. Put the apples and the vinegar in a large, heavy-bottomed preserving pan and boil gently for 5 minutes to soften the apples. Add the green tomatoes, then bring back to the boil, lower the heat and simmer for a further 10 minutes.

4. Add the garlic, salt, chilli and roasted spices and give it a good stir, then add the sugars. Bring back to a gentle boil and stir until all the sugar has dissolved.

5. Add the chopped dates; the mixture will thicken quite quickly. Boil for another 20 minutes, or until the correct consistency is reached, stirring regularly to stop the chutney catching on the base of the pan. Test by running a spoon along the bottom of the pan – if the channel you make doesn't fill immediately, the chutney is ready.

6. Remove the pan from the heat, spoon the chutney into sterilised jars and seal immediately. Store for two months before using.

Mango chutney

The granddaddy of all the chutneys, this is resplendently sweet. No curry is complete without it. To be truly authentic, it must be made from green mangoes, which are hard and sour but hold their shape and texture. They are widely available from Indian supermarkets. The more common Alphonse mango will disintegrate and create a chutney without the chunks of fruit.

Makes 3–5 jars

900g (2lb) green mangoes, halved, peeled, stoned and cut into chunks

½ tsp sea salt

300ml (10fl oz or 1¼ cups) cider vinegar

225g (8oz) or approximately 2 medium Bramley apples, peeled, cored and cut into pieces

1 clove of garlic, peeled and crushed

1½ tbsp ground ginger

200g (7oz or 1 cup) raw cane sugar

1. Put the chopped mangoes in a bowl, sprinkle with the salt and mix. Set aside for 10 minutes.

2. Heat the vinegar in a large, heavy-bottomed preserving pan. Add the mangoes and apples and bring to the boil. Lower the heat and simmer for 15 minutes to soften.

3. Add the garlic and ground ginger, bring back to the boil, then add the sugar and stir continuously until it has completely dissolved. Continue to boil for 30 minutes, or until the desired consistency is reached, stirring regularly to stop the chutney catching on the base of the pan. Test by running a spoon along the bottom of the pan – if the channel you make doesn't fill immediately, the chutney is ready.

4. Remove the pan from the heat, pour the chutney into sterilised jars and seal immediately. Store for two months before using.

Spicy variation
Adding chilli and lightly toasted spices will give the chutney some heat.

1. Preheat the oven to 200°C/400°F/gas mark 6. Spread 1 heaped teaspoon each of cumin seeds and coriander seeds over a baking tray. Bake in the oven for 2 minutes, remove the tray and shake the seeds, then toast for another 2 minutes. Lightly crush the seeds with a pestle and mortar, just enough to crack them open.

Fruit & nut variation
You can also add dried fruits and nuts at the same time as the garlic and ginger in step 3. We recommend 25g (1oz) of a mix of roughly chopped cashews and pistachios or almonds with 20g (¾oz) of chopped dates and sultanas and/or raisins.

2. Meanwhile, deseed and finely chop 1 fresh red chilli, mix it with the seeds and add to the chutney right at the end of the cooking process. The spices will work their magic in the jar and create another dimension to mango chutney.

Date & apple chutney

This fine example of a typical Kashmir chutney was given to us by the winner of the chutney-making competition at Chutfest, an event that celebrates the art of chutney-making. This recipe was passed down to Teresa from her grandmother, and takes full advantage of the practice of adding exotic fruits to English fruits. Historically it would have been made at Christmas time, when large country houses might find themselves with a surfeit of leftover dried dates.

Makes 4–6 jars

1.5kg (3lb 5oz) or approximately 8 Bramley apples, peeled, cored and chopped

500g (1lb 2oz) or approximately 3 onions, peeled and finely chopped

500g (1lb 2oz or 3 cups) dried seedless dates, finely chopped

1 heaped tsp sea salt

2 tsp ground ginger

2 tsp ground cinnamon

½ tsp cayenne pepper

300ml (10fl oz or 1¼ cups) cider vinegar

500g (1lb 2oz or 2½ cups) demerara sugar

1. Put the apples, onions, dates, salt and spices in a large, heavy-bottomed preserving pan and add half the vinegar. Heat slowly, stirring continuously, and bring to a gentle boil. Lower the heat and simmer for 30 minutes until everything is soft.

2. Stir in the sugar and the remaining vinegar and continue to stir until all the sugar has dissolved. Bring back to the boil and continue boiling for about 20 minutes, or until the correct consistency is reached, stirring frequently to stop the chutney catching on the base of the pan. Test by running a spoon along the bottom of the pan – if the channel you make doesn't fill immediately, the chutney is ready.

3. Remove the pan from the heat, pour the chutney into sterilised jars and seal immediately. Store for two months before using.

Pear, walnut & perry chutney

Making the most of some slightly under-ripe windfall pears, a bag of walnuts leftover from Christmas and a gift of some perry, we came up with this recipe, which we think is delicious with crumbly cheese. It is a truly delicious way of making something wonderful out of what would otherwise be inedible. You need to cook this chutney for longer than normal because it will be watered down at the end with the perry.

Makes 4–6 jars

100g (3½oz or 1 cup) walnuts

300g (10½oz or 2 cups) onions, peeled and diced

250ml (9fl oz or 1 cup + 2 tbsp) cider vinegar

350g (12oz) or approximately 2 Bramley apples, peeled, cored and chopped into 1-cm (½-inch) cubes

1kg (2lb 4oz or approximately 6–7) pears, peeled, cored and chopped into 1-cm (½-inch) cubes

250g (9oz or 1¼ cups) raw cane sugar

250g (9oz or 1¼ cups) muscovado sugar

200g (7oz or 1⅓ cups) sultanas

1 tsp ground ginger

½ tsp yellow mustard seeds

1 tsp ground cinnamon

½ fresh red chilli, deseeded and finely chopped

Juice of ½ lemon

1 tbsp sea salt

250ml (9fl oz or 1 cup + 2 tbsp) perry

1. Preheat the oven to 175°C/350°F/gas mark 3–4.

2. Spread the walnuts on a baking tray and toast them for 8–10 minutes, shaking once during that time. Then take them out and allow them to cool before chopping into pieces.

3. Put the onions and vinegar in a large, heavy-bottomed preserving pan. Bring to the boil, then lower the heat and simmer for 5 minutes, or until the onion has softened.

4. Add the apples and pears and simmer for a further 5 minutes before adding the sugars, sultanas, spices, chilli, lemon juice and salt. Stir really well to make sure all the sugar has dissolved and boil for 30 minutes or so, stirring frequently to stop the chutney catching on the base of the pan. Test by running a spoon along the bottom of the pan – if the channel you make doesn't fill immediately, the chutney is ready.

5. Once you're happy that you've got the correct consistency, remove the pan from the heat, add the perry and the walnuts, and give it a final good stir to make sure they are well mixed in. If you think the chutney is too runny, you can put it back on the heat to reduce it further, but bear in mind that heating at this point will cook off the alcohol.

6. Spoon the chutney into sterilised jars and seal immediately. Store for two months before using.

Apple & cider brandy chutney

Once, while visiting Julian Temperley of the Somerset Cider Brandy Company in his Somerset orchards, Guy and Julian enjoyed an early evening glass of cider brandy and a good chat while watching the sun set hazily over the rows of apple trees. That magical setting inspired this chutney, which is a melding of two great traditions: chutney-making and cider-making. The addition of a third great British ingredient, Cheddar, makes the perfect picnic plate.

Makes 4–6 jars

1kg (2lb 4oz) or about 3 Bramley apples, peeled and cored and chopped

3 medium onions, peeled and finely chopped

350ml (12fl oz or 1½ cups) cider vinegar

4 cloves of garlic, peeled and crushed

1 tsp ground ginger

1 tsp ground cinnamon

1 tsp ground allspice

1 fresh red chilli, deseeded and finely chopped

4 tsp sea salt

500g (1lb 2oz or 2½ cups) raw cane sugar

170g (6oz or scant 1 cup) muscovado sugar

150g (5½oz or 1 cup) sultanas

25ml (1 tbsp + 2 tsp) cider brandy or dry cider

1. Put the apples, onions and vinegar in a large, heavy-bottomed preserving pan and bring to the boil, stirring frequently. When they're boiling nicely, add the garlic, spices, chilli and salt and stir to mix well.

2. Slowly add the sugars, stirring to ensure that they are completely dissolved, then add the sultanas. Bring back to the boil for 30–40 minutes, or until the chutney has reached the right consistency, stirring regularly to stop the chutney catching on the base of the pan. Test by running a spoon along the bottom of the pan – if the channel you make doesn't fill immediately, the chutney is ready.

3. Remove the pan from the heat, stir in the cider brandy or cider, and spoon into sterilised jars. Seal immediately and store for two months before using.

Country garden chutney

This recipe comes from Guy's great-grandmother who would have been very proud to know that her chutney recipe is still a stalwart of her great-grandson's condiments company. With 20 ingredients, it tops the chart and really is a collection of every vegetable left in her kitchen garden. It admirably demonstrates that chutneys are incredibly useful for using up any glut of fresh fruit or vegetables.

Makes 3–5 jars

150g (5½oz or scant 1 cup) dried apricots

450g (1lb) vegetables, peeled and cut into 1-cm (½-inch) cubes; we use:
130g (4½oz) carrots
120g (4oz) swede
100g (3½oz) turnips
100g (3½oz) parsnips

120g (4oz) Bramley apples, peeled and chopped

2 large onions, peeled and chopped

300ml (10fl oz or 1¼ cups) cider vinegar

35g (1¼oz or 2 tbsp) sea salt

600g (1lb 5oz or 3 cups) raw cane sugar

100g (3½oz) tomatoes, chopped

20ml (4 tsp) tamarind paste

35g (1¼oz or 7 cloves) garlic, peeled and crushed

1 heaped tbsp ground ginger

¼ tsp ground cinnamon

½ tsp ground allspice

Large pinch of freshly ground black pepper

1 heaped tbsp mustard powder

1 fresh red chilli, deseeded and very finely chopped

50g (1¾oz or ⅓ cup) sultanas

1. Put the apricots in a heatproof bowl and add 150ml (5fl oz or ⅔ cup) of boiling water. Leave to soak for about 30 minutes while you prepare the rest of the ingredients.

2. Put the cubed vegetables, apples, onions and vinegar in a large, heavy-bottomed preserving pan and bring to the boil. Add the salt, lower the heat and simmer for 5 minutes, or until the vegetables are softening. Don't let them become mushy.

3. Stir in the sugar and continue stirring until it has completely dissolved. Add the rest of the ingredients, including the apricots and their water, and bring back to the boil.

4. Continue to boil for about 20 minutes until the correct consistency is reached, stirring regularly to stop the chutney catching on the base of the pan. Test by running a spoon along the bottom of the pan – if the channel you make doesn't fill immediately, the chutney is ready.

5. Remove the pan from the heat, spoon into sterilised jars and seal immediately. Store for two months before using.

Roasted shallot & garlic chutney

On holiday in Italy and inspired by the beautiful flavours of the food, Guy decided to experiment with roasting shallots and garlic, making a chutney that was at once hot and mellow. He liked the result so much that on the return journey he jettisoned some non-essential clothes from his suitcase, packing the jars instead so that everyone at Tracklements could taste his efforts. Thank goodness the customs officials didn't open his suitcase...

Makes 4–6 jars

100ml (3½fl oz or scant ½ cup) olive oil

1kg (2lb 4oz) shallots, topped, tailed and peeled

200g (7oz or approximately 6½ heads) garlic, peeled

600g (1lb 5oz or 3 cups) muscovado sugar

400ml (14fl oz or 1¾ cups) cider vinegar

100ml (3½fl oz or scant ½ cup) balsamic vinegar

1 fresh red chilli, deseeded and finely chopped

25g (1oz or 1½ tbsp) sea salt

Pinch of freshly ground black pepper

1. Preheat the oven to 180°C/350°F/gas mark 4.

2. Pour the olive oil into a large roasting dish, add the shallots and garlic and toss in the oil until well-coated. Put on the top shelf of the oven and roast for 45 minutes, turning regularly until golden brown, soft and squishy.

3. Transfer the shallots and garlic into a large, heavy-bottomed preserving pan and add 120g (4oz or ½ cup) of the sugar. Heat gently and stir continuously to stop the sugar catching on the base of the pan.

4. Turn the heat up slowly; the shallots will start to break up and the sugar will caramelise. When you're happy that the sugar has started to caramelise add the vinegars, chilli, salt and pepper.

5. Stir well and add the rest of the sugar. Bring the mixture to the boil, lower the heat and simmer gently for 20 minutes, or until the desired consistency is reached, stirring regularly to stop the chutney catching on the base of the pan. Test by running a spoon along the bottom of the pan – if the channel you make doesn't fill immediately, the chutney is ready.

6. Remove the pan from the heat, spoon into sterilised jars and seal immediately. Store for two months before using.

Pumpkin & orange chutney

The smell of this chutney being made conjures up images of golden, autumnal leaves, a blazing fire and frosty fingers wrapped around a sausage in a bun. Delicate and mild pumpkin is given a leg up by warming chillies and fresh-tasting orange zest. This is a chutney guaranteed to ward off the winter blues.

Makes 4–6 jars

1kg (2lb 4oz) pumpkin, peeled and chopped into 1-cm (½-inch) cubes

300g (10½oz) or approximately 2 Bramley apples, peeled, cored and chopped

2 small onions, peeled and diced

600ml (20fl oz or 2½ cups) cider vinegar

400g (14oz or 2 cups) raw cane sugar

30g (1oz or about 2½ tbsp) sultanas

grated orange zest of 1 orange

50g (1¾oz or approximately 10) fresh red chillies, deseeded and finely chopped

5g (⅛oz) fresh ginger root, peeled and very finely diced

2 tsp sea salt

1. Put the pumpkin, apples, onions and vinegar into a large, heavy-bottomed preserving pan. Heat on a medium heat for 10 minutes until soft.

2. Bring the mixture to the boil. Add the sugar, sultanas, orange zest, chillies, ginger and salt. Stir well to ensure all the sugar is dissolved and the other ingredients are evenly distributed.

3. Boil for about 20 minutes, stirring frequently to make sure the chutney doesn't catch on the base of the pan, until the correct consistency is achieved. Test by running a spoon along the bottom of the pan – if the channel you make doesn't fill immediately, the chutney is ready.

4. Remove the pan from the heat and spoon the chutney into sterilised jars. Seal immediately and store for two months before using.

MUSTARDS

'The thought of a sausage without putting a dollop of wholegrain mustard all over it – no, no. I couldn't live with that.'
Guy Tullberg, 2010

From ancient times to the present day, mustard has always been a highly prized and sought-after spice. There are references to it in ancient Egyptian, Greek and Roman texts, and it is mentioned in the Bible several times. The mustard plant was introduced to Britain by the Romans. Cherished by them for its medicinal qualities as well as for its ability to make unappetising meat palatable, no self-respecting Roman travelled without a pouch of mustard to plant. It grows impressively easily and quickly and such are its reproductive qualities that the Hindus use mustard seed as a symbol of fertility. A small handful of mustard seed (20g/¾oz) will produce three sacks of seeds in two summers. The Romans ground the seed by crushing it and mixing it with verjuice or grape must (mustum). They called the resultant seedy paste *mustum ardens* ('fiery' or 'burning must') which is how we get the word 'mustard'. The Roman version of this condiment was very similar to the wholegrain mustards we know today.

Such was the popularity of this fiery concoction that in Tudor England every monastery had a mustardarius: someone responsible for growing and distributing mustard. Its popularity was assured both because of its culinary uses and also because of the belief that it could help cure all manner of ills, including pneumonia, poor circulation, sore joints, memory loss, toothaches, skin problems and stomach ache and it was even used as a cure for hiccups. Mustard seed was used in drinks as a love potion, in poultices to encourage sweating and stimulate healing, in plasters to get rid of boils and in the bath to cure colds and flu.

The first inklings of the English commercial trade in mustards were in Tewkesbury in the mid-17th century, where the seed was pounded, mixed with water and shaped into balls that were dried to be sold at markets. These mustard balls were taken home and reconstituted with vinegar to make the condiment mustard. Not until the 18th century did Mrs Clements of Durham first grind mustard in a mill and then sift it to make mustard 'flour.' This hot, bright-yellow culinary gem quickly became the fashion – consequently some of the more enterprising millers started to put their grindstones to milling mustard instead of wheat flour. In the mid-18th century the Keen & Sons mustard company was established in London, and by the mid-19th century, smooth mustards made from mustard flour began to dominate.

Such was the popularity of strong English mustard that wholegrain mustards were no longer made. They largely fell out of public consciousness until 1970, when a young William Tullberg found a recipe for a wholegrain mustard in John Evelyn's 17th-century *Acetaria: A Discourse of Sallets*:

'That the seeds should be pounded in a mortar, or bruised with a polish'd cannon bullet, in a large wooden bowl dish, or which is most prefer'd, ground in a quern contriv'd for this purpose only.'

William was intrigued, and thanks to his unquenchable thirst for experimenting, he pressed an old coffee grinder into service and wholegrain mustard-production in Britain was revived.

Making mustards

Wholegrain mustard is simple to make and infinitely variable, and its strength and flavour are entirely a matter of personal taste. Everyone reacts to the spice's heat individually, so by making your own, you can tailor it to suit your palate.

The aim is to make a condiment that will stimulate your taste buds without overpowering the main part of the meal. Jeremiah Colman, founder of the Colman mustard firm, claimed that his fortune was made by what people left on the side of their plates, but we want every last scrap of our wholegrain mustards devoured with not a seed left behind!

Yellow and brown mustard seeds, dried bird's-eye chillies, allspice, peppercorns and vinegar, along with some time and a good deal of patience, are the key ingredients to creating this versatile condiment.

The mustard plant is part of the *Brassicaceae* (or older name of *Cruciferae*) family and is related to radishes, cresses, and in particular cabbages and other brassicas. When chewed, the yellow seed (*Sinapsis alba*) gives a warm, peppery flavour with a slight sweetness combined with a nuttiness and heat in the mouth and along the tongue. Mustard is mainly grown in North America, but the dried seeds can be bought online or from health-food shops.

The brown seed (*Brassica juncea*), on the other hand, yields a flavour that goes up the nose, and leaves a slightly bitter taste in the mouth. All Tracklements' mustards use a combination of these two seeds in varying proportions, depending on the end flavour we want to achieve.

'Wholegrain' is in fact a misnomer; whole mustard seeds are essentially tasteless. It is only when the seed shell is opened that it releases its flavour, so the key to making wholegrain mustard is in the grinding of the seed. To create a genuine wholegrain, the seed must be gently 'kissed' by the grinding stones rather than ground to powder, but there are several different textures that fall between these two extremes; sometimes we may grind the seed more than once to achieve a smoother consistency.

We always recommend using whole spices and grinding them with the mustard seeds as this retains the essential oils that give the mustard its depth of flavour. When grinding, you can use a pestle and mortar for authenticity – and to build up your muscles! Alternatively, you can use a stick blender, in which case you need to choose a high-sided bowl so that the mustard seeds don't fly out everywhere. A retired coffee grinder also works well.

Mustard acts as a natural preservative, which is why it's so often used as an ingredient in pickling, but in order to keep made mustard at its best, both vinegar and salt are also required. As with all these things the vinegar plays such an important role that a good one is essential to the end taste. As a very general rule of thumb, homemade mustards require just over double the amount of liquid to ground seeds when first made. The liquid is then soaked up by the ground mustard seeds over a period of time. If your mustard seems too dry, you can always add more vinegar to loosen it.

All mustards need time to mellow and mature, so make sure you plan ahead. Mustard is too raw to eat when it has just been made. Wholegrain mustards should be allowed to stand in a covered bowl for four days and stirred regularly. Be careful when you stir it every day – we recommend you don't lean over the bowl too much or you may find yourself adding your own brand of salt water to the recipe!

If you are cooking with smooth mustards such as Dijon and strong English, add them only at the very end of the cooking process; otherwise they will add a bitter flavour. A wholegrain mustard can happily be used at the beginning of the cooking process without losing its flavour.

Wholegrain mustard

Makes 3–5 small jars

100g (3½oz) yellow mustard seeds

140g (5oz) brown mustard seeds

½ tsp black peppercorns

3 allspice berries

approximately 6 dried bird's-eye chillies or 1 tsp dried crushed chillies

350ml (12fl oz or 1½ cups) cider vinegar

230ml (8fl oz or 1 cup) water

2 tsp sea salt

The resurgence of the decent sausage is one of the great stories of the last 20 years and this mustard makes a perfect partner. A really tremendous allrounder, it provides a gentle heat and a real front of the mouth 'punch' and is as good stirred into a recipe as it is on the side of the plate. Its gentle nuttiness also makes it perfect for livening up mashed potato or a cheese sauce.

1. Grind the mustard seeds and spices until a coarse grind is achieved.

2. Mix together the vinegar, water and salt and stir to dissolve the salt. Add this liquid to the grind. Give it a good stir – it will look thin and very liquid at this point. Cover and leave to stand overnight.

3. The next day, give the mixture a further stir; it should be thickening up nicely. Cover and leave overnight again. Repeat this process twice more, until the mustard has thickened up. Spoon into sterilised jars and seal immediately.

Lemon mustard

Makes 3–5 small jars

350ml (12fl oz or 1½ cups) cider vinegar

200ml (7fl oz or scant 1 cup) water

2 tsp sea salt

2 tsp raw cane sugar

1 lemon (30ml or 2 tbsp juice, lemon zest and 15g or ½oz lemon pulp)

125g (4½oz) yellow mustard seeds

125g (4½oz) brown mustard seeds

1 tsp black peppercorns

approximately 6 dried bird's-eye chillies or 1 tsp dried crushed chillies

Delicious with turkey or chicken, the lemon adds sharpness to the mustard. We use this mustard to add zing to mayonnaise and it naturally complements summer roast chicken with a green salad.

1. Put the vinegar, water, salt and sugar into a bowl and give a good stir to dissolve the salt and sugar. Add the lemon juice, zest and pulp. Cover and leave overnight.

2. Grind the mustard seeds and spices until a coarse grind is achieved, then add to the vinegar mixture and stir well. Cover and leave to stand overnight.

3. The next day give the mixture a further stir and cover again. Repeat daily for up to seven days. Allowing it to mature this long should produce a good, rounded flavour. Then spoon into sterilised jars and seal immediately.

Green peppercorn mustard

Makes 3–5 small jars

150g (5½oz) yellow mustard seeds

85g (3oz) brown mustard seeds

1 tbsp green peppercorns in their brine

1 tsp black peppercorns

1 tsp (approximately 18) allspice berries

approximately 6 dried bird's-eye chillies or 1 tsp dried crushed chillies

230ml (8fl oz or 1 cup) water

340ml (12fl oz or 1½ cups) cider vinegar

2 tsp sea salt

An excellent mustard for spreading onto any meat before cooking or grilling but we think it's especially good with steak. The green peppercorns give a really lovely vibrancy to the taste.

1. Using a pestle and mortar, grind the mustard seeds, green and black peppercorns, allspice and chillies together to a fine grind.

2. Put the water, vinegar and salt into a large bowl, add the ground mustard seed mixture and stir.

3. Leave the mixture to mature for up to five days, stirring daily and covering in between. Give the mixture a short whizz with your stick blender, adding a couple of tablespoons of vinegar if necessary. Spoon into sterilised jars and seal immediately.

Spiced honey mustard

Makes 3–5 small jars

110g (3¾oz) yellow mustard seeds

110g (3¾oz) brown mustard seeds

½ tsp black peppercorns

6 allspice berries

approximately 4 dried bird's-eye chillies or 1 tsp dried crushed chillies

275g (9½oz or 1⅓ cups) mustard flour

620ml (22fl oz or 2¾ cups) cider vinegar

200ml (7fl oz or 1 scant cup) sunflower oil

280ml (9½fl oz or 1⅓ cups) runny honey

140g raw cane sugar

A no nonsense, powerhouse of a mustard! This mustard will go right up the nose and clear the head. The first taste is the sweetness of the honey followed by the pungency of the mustard and finally the heat. Spiced Honey Mustard is our favourite for glazing a Wiltshire ham or using to bring mini sausage rolls to life.

1. Grind the mustard seeds and spices together to a coarse grind, i.e. until the grind looks like freshly ground pepper.

2. Mix in the mustard flour and ensure it is evenly distributed. Add the vinegar and mix well before adding the sunflower oil, honey and sugar and mixing as well. Whizz the mustard using a stick blender for a further 30 seconds.

3. Spoon into sterilised jars and seal immediately. Wait at least a week before opening to allow the flavour to develop.

Tarragon mustard

Makes 3–5 small jars

140g (5oz) yellow mustard seeds

140g (5oz) brown mustard seeds

1 tsp black peppercorns

approximately 6 dried bird's-eye chillies or 1 tsp dried crushed chillies

25g (1oz) fresh tarragon leaves, washed and very finely chopped

430ml (15fl oz or scant 2 cups) cider vinegar

170ml (6fl oz or ¾ cup) water

2 rounded tsp sea salt

This is one of my favourites. Taste this mustard and let the flavours roll round your mouth. The tarragon makes this mustard reminiscent of a classic 'Meaux' grainy mustard. It is very good with white meats and fish dishes.

1. Grind the mustard seeds, peppercorns and chillies to a fine grind.

2. Add the tarragon to the ground mustard seed, along with the vinegar, water and sea salt.

3. Stir well, cover and leave to stand overnight. The next day give the mixture a further stir and cover again. Repeat the process for 5–7 days. Check that the consistency is right – a few more tablespoons of vinegar may be added at this stage if you feel it is too thick. Then put into sterilised jars and seal immediately.

Beer mustard

Makes 4–6 small jars

200ml (7fl oz or 1 scant cup) bitter beer (not lager)

2 tsp sea salt

140g (5oz) yellow mustard seeds

140g (5oz) brown mustard seeds

1 tsp black peppercorns

1 tsp (approximately 18) allspice berries

approximately 6 dried bird's-eye chillies or 1 tsp dried crushed chillies

450ml (16fl oz or 2 cups) cider vinegar

The addition of beer gives a strong malty aroma to the mustard which makes it ideal for adding to a good, strong Cheddar cheese when making the perfect cheese on toast. Enjoy this mustard also with a sausage or a pork pie.

1. Open the beer, add the salt to it, stir and leave overnight. This allows the beer to go flat so that its bubbles don't react with the mustard seed.

2. The next day, grind the mustard seeds, spices and chillies until you have a coarse grind. Pour the beer into a bowl, stir to make sure that the salt has dissolved, then add the vinegar and the mustard mixture and stir.

3. Cover and leave to mature for 3–4 days, stirring daily so that the mustard soaks up the liquid. Cover between the stirs. Spoon into sterilised jars and seal immediately.

Mostarda

A classic and flamboyant Italian condiment made with fruit and mustard seed and preserved with sugar, *mostarda* falls somewhere between a relish and a mustard. We've included it here because of its close association with mustard. This version uses traditional English fruit to make a deliciously piquant relish for cold meats.

Makes 4–6 jars

250ml (9fl oz or 1 cup + 2 tbsp) water

250g (9oz or 1¼ cups) raw cane sugar

2 tsp yellow mustard seeds

200g (7oz) or approximately 1 quince, peeled, cored and chopped into large pieces

200g (7oz) approximately 1 pear, peeled, cored and chopped into large pieces

200g (7oz) or approximately 1 dessert apple, peeled, cored and chopped into large pieces

100g (3½oz or ⅔ cup) dried figs, finely chopped

2 tsp mustard powder

1. Make the sugar syrup by putting the water, sugar and mustard seeds into a large pan and heating, stirring continuously until all the sugar has dissolved. Bring to the boil for 5–10 minutes.

2. Add the chopped quince and boil for 5 minutes, then add the chopped pear and boil for a further 5 minutes. Add the chopped apple and boil for 5 minutes before adding the finely chopped figs. Give the mixture a gentle stir, lower the heat and simmer for a further 10 minutes.

3. Remove from heat and stir in the mustard powder so it is well mixed in before spooning the mixture into sterilised jars. Make sure that all the fruit is covered with the syrup. Seal immediately.

Rocket hot mustard

Makes 4–6 small jars

420g (15oz) mustard powder

500ml (18fl oz or 2¼ cups) water

80ml (3fl oz or ⅓ cup) cider vinegar

60g (2¼oz) or 3 heaped tbsp sea salt

4 tsp chilli powder

3 tbsp ground turmeric

125g (4½ oz or ½ cup) raw cane sugar

This mustard packs an honest and forthright punch. It's hot, really hot, so use sparingly to add a wallop to a sandwich.

1. Put all the ingredients into a blender (or deep-sided bowl if you're using a stick blender) and whizz together for 30 seconds. Scrape the sides to make sure everything is evenly mixed and whizz again for 10 seconds.

2. Spoon into sterilised jars and seal immediately.

Fresh chilli mustard

Makes 3–5 small jars

70g (2½oz) yellow mustard seeds

175g (6oz) brown mustard seeds

1 tsp black peppercorns

1 tsp (approximately 18) allspice berries

approximately 6 dried bird's-eye chillies or 1 tsp dried crushed chillies

360ml (12fl oz or 1½ cups) cider vinegar

120ml (4fl oz or ½ cup) water

65g (2¼oz or just under 5 tbsp) runny honey

20g (¾oz or 4 tsp) sea salt

20g (¾oz or 4 tsp) raw cane sugar

3 fresh red chillies, deseeded

The poke and heat of this fiery mustard will add depth and dimension to everything with which it's served. Ideal mixed with mayo to make a relish for burgers.

1. Grind the mustard seeds, spices and chillies together to a fine grind.

2. Put the cider vinegar, water, honey, salt and sugar into a large bowl and stir until the honey, sugar and salt have dissolved. Add the ground mustard seed mixture and stir.

3. Use a stick blender to whizz the red chillies, or dice them very finely and add to the mustard. Cover and leave the mustard mixture to mature for up to three days, stirring each day and covering in between. Spoon into sterilised jars and seal immediately.

Tewkesbury mustard

Makes 3–5 small jars

95g (3½oz) yellow mustard seeds

95g (3½oz) brown mustard seeds

½ tsp black peppercorns

½ tsp (approximately 9) allspice berries

approximately 3 dried bird's-eye chillies or ½ tsp dried crushed chillies

4 tsp mustard powder

110g (4oz) fresh horseradish root

320ml (11fl oz or 1⅓ cups) cider vinegar

160ml (5½fl oz or scant ¾ cup) water

2 tsp sea salt

The natural mustard to partner beef whether hot or cold. It's hard to imagine Beef Wellington without it.

1. Grind the mustard seeds, spices and chillies together to a fine grind. Mix in the mustard powder and ensure it is evenly distributed. Put to one side.

2. Grate the horseradish root (this is less painful on the eyes if the root has been left to chill in the fridge for an hour beforehand), then blitz using a stick blender to get rid of any lumps.

3. Put the cider vinegar, water and salt into a large bowl and stir until the salt has dissolved, then add the horseradish.

4. Add the ground mustard seed mixture and give a thorough stir. Cover the mixture and leave overnight.

5. Leave the mixture to mature for up to three days, stirring daily and covering in between. Finally give the mustard a quick blitz with a stick blender before spooning into sterilised jars. Seal immediately.

Honey mustard

Makes 3–5 small jars

70g (2½oz) yellow mustard seeds

200g (7oz) brown mustard seeds

1 tsp black peppercorns

approximately 6 dried bird's-eye chillies or 1 tsp dried crushed chillies

380ml (13fl oz or generous 1½ cups) cider vinegar

150ml (5fl oz or ⅔ cup) water

70g (2½oz or approximately 5 tbsp) runny honey

2 tsp sea salt

Mustard with cheese is so often overlooked, but this beautifully mellow mustard is perfect with grilled halloumi. It is equally good in white sauce for cauliflower and leek dishes.

1. Grind the mustard seeds, peppercorns and chillies to a fine grind.

2. Put the cider vinegar, water, honey and salt into a large bowl and stir until the honey and salt have dissolved. Add the ground mustard seed mixture and stir.

3. Leave the mixture to mature for up to four days, stirring each day and covering in between. Spoon into sterilised jars and seal immediately.

RELISHES

'Think big thoughts but relish small pleasures.'
H Jackson Brown, Jr, *Life's Little Instruction Book*, 1991

We think of relishes as the Johnny-come-latelys of the condiment kingdom. When we are asked by customers the difference between relishes, pickles and chutneys we frequently reply that relishes are those pickles and chutneys that the Pilgrim Fathers took with them when they left Britain and which came back across the Atlantic generations later as relishes.

It's really not quite that simple, though. Relishes are more often than not a combination of both pickles and chutneys. They seem to embody both the pickle-eater's desire for crunch and the chutney-lover's melding of flavours and spicing. Relishes, we believe, owe their existence less to the historical need to preserve a seasonal glut and more to the love of flavour and garnish that they exemplify. Even their name implies enthusiasm, and it's not clear which use came first: the noun or the verb. Their heritage is less functional necessity and more celebratory exuberance.

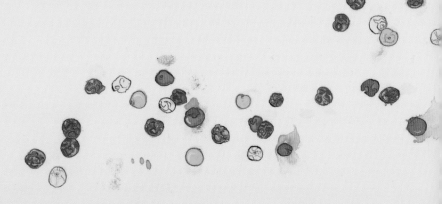

They are the teenagers of the condiment world, and as such, they break – or rather, 'bend' – some of the traditional rules of preserving: for example, they generally have a shorter cooking time.

Because they are more modern, relishes use lots of ingredients creatively. They typically make good use of chilli to add a little poke. They tend to be fresher in flavour, brighter in colour and tangier in taste. In keeping with the enthusiasm they portray, we think of relishes as accompaniments that are used in generous dollops rather than small quantities. These recipes should get lips smacking together in anticipation – one might even say, with relish!

In this chapter we have collected together those recipes that don't quite sit comfortably with being called either a pickle or a chutney. We have adapted the following recipes to ensure the balance of sugar and vinegar is such that the products will keep for six months if stored in the fridge.

Making relishes

The aim is to make a product with a short cooking time that will create a fresh, bright flavour retaining the original taste of whatever fruit or vegetable has been used. Generally relishes are cooked just long enough to preserve. Think preserves for the impatient.

The sugar is often added earlier in the process than in chutney- or pickle-making to maintain a fresh zing to the relish. A shorter cooking time means less evaporation of liquid, so relishes sometimes make use of cornflour to help thicken the sauce around the vegetables.

Like their predecessors, relishes use a combination of sugar, vinegar, fruit or vegetables, salt and spices. Chilli is nearly always present in modern-day relishes to give a burst of heat. Some relishes can also contain a lower proportion of vinegar and sugar, which means that they will not keep for as long. For this reason, they are usually made and consumed within a shorter space of time. Whereas chutneys and pickles should be left alone for a minimum of two months, these relishes should be enjoyed within two months.

The fruit and vegetables used in making relishes are usually cut into smaller, neater pieces. Relishes are all about convenience, modern eating habits and exceptionally vibrant flavours.

Chilli jam

People have written odes to our chilli jam, eaten it straight from the jar and used it to pep up a multitude of dishes. It has been paired with fish, cheese, meat and even ice cream! A person's tolerance to chilli is as individual as their fingerprints, so while some people may think this is a mild condiment, others will find their eyes watering and their lips tingling. Making your own will ensure that you tailor it to your own personal taste.

Makes 3–5 jars

1 medium onion, peeled and roughly chopped

415g (14½oz) or approximately 5 red peppers, deseeded and roughly chopped

330ml (11fl oz or 1⅓ cups) cider vinegar

835g (1lb 13¼oz or 4¼ cups) raw cane sugar

60ml (4 tbsp) lemon juice

3 cloves of garlic, peeled and crushed

1 tsp sea salt

415g (14½oz) or approximately 85 red chillies, deseeded and finely chopped

1. Whizz the onion and red peppers in a food processor for 10 seconds.

2. Warm the vinegar in a large, heavy-based preserving pan and add the onion and peppers. Bring to the boil, lower the heat and simmer for 5 minutes, then add the sugar, stirring until it has dissolved. Stir in the lemon juice.

3. Add the garlic, salt and chillies to the pan. Bring to the boil, stirring frequently. Keep at a rolling boil for between 30–40 minutes until the mixture has thickened to a good consistency. Spoon into sterilised jars and seal immediately.

Green chilli jam

Green chillies are milder than their red counterparts and they have a different heat, which is why we introduced this chilli jam to our range in 2010. To differentiate it further we have added ginger, lime and coriander, with a splash of tamari sauce. We think it is a really sophisticated relish that goes brilliantly with fish and cold chicken.

We use tamari, a type of soy sauce made without wheat that enables this recipe to be gluten-free. It is available from specialist delis and grocers, but if you can't get hold of any, you can substitute soy sauce.

Makes 3–5 jars

1 medium onion, peeled and roughly chopped

3–4 green peppers, chopped into 1-cm (½-inch) pieces

20g (¾oz) fresh ginger root, peeled and roughly chopped

4 cloves of garlic, peeled and crushed

250ml (9fl oz or 1 cup + 2 tbsp) cider vinegar

835g (1lb 13¼oz or 4¼ cups) raw cane sugar

60ml (4 tbsp) lemon juice

10ml (2 tsp) lime juice

20ml (4 tsp) tamari sauce

210g (7oz) or approximately 42 green chillies, deseeded and finely chopped

1 tsp sea salt

1 small handful fresh coriander, washed and finely chopped

1. Whizz together the onion, green peppers, ginger and garlic for 10 seconds, until the pieces are about 2mm (¹⁄₁₆ inch) in size; you are not trying to take it down to a purée.

2. Warm the vinegar in a large, heavy-bottomed preserving saucepan. Add the onion mixture and then bring to a gentle simmer for 5 minutes. Then add the sugar, stirring continuously until it has completely dissolved.

3. Add the lemon juice, lime juice and tamari sauce and stir.

4. Add the chillies and salt. Bring to the boil, stirring frequently. Keep at a rolling boil for between 30–40 minutes until the mixture has thickened to a good consistency. Remove from the heat.

5. Add the finely chopped coriander and stir. Spoon into sterilised jars and seal immediately.

Caramelised onion marmalade

Tracklements introduced the very first onion marmalade commercially available in the UK back in the late 1990s. At the time it was so unique that Trading Standards questioned whether we could legally call it a marmalade, but Sir Kenelm Digby and his 17th-century recipe for a 'marmulate' of onions came to our rescue! Cooked like any marmalade, this product should have a firm set once cool. It's one of the longest to prepare but worth every tear! We recommend using white onions as they're sweeter than red ones when caramelised.

Makes 4–6 jars

For the spiced vinegar

10 whole cloves

Pinch of ground ginger

1 cinnamon quill

150ml (5fl oz or ⅔ cup) cider vinegar

For the onion marmalade

1.5kg (3lb 5oz) or 9–10 onions, peeled and sliced

30ml (2 tbsp) olive oil

100g (3½oz) redcurrant jelly

250g (9oz or 1¼ cups) raw cane sugar

1 tsp lemon juice

1. Make a spiced vinegar by putting the cloves, ground ginger, cinnamon quill and cider vinegar in a large saucepan. Heat to a simmer, then remove from the heat and leave to infuse for an hour while preparing the onions.

2. Add the onions and olive oil to a large, heavy-bottomed preserving pan and cook very gently for 30–40 minutes until the slices are transparent.

3. Remove and discard the cloves and cinnamon quill from the vinegar mixture. Add the vinegar to the onions, simmering for 5–10 minutes to reduce.

4. Add the redcurrant jelly and allow it to melt, then add the sugar and stir gently over the heat until all the sugar has dissolved – be careful not to let it catch on the bottom of the pan.

5. Add the lemon juice and boil for an hour or so, until the correct consistency is reached. Test by runninging a spoon along the bottom of the pan – if the channel you make doesn't fill immediately, the relish is ready. Spoon into sterilised jars and seal immediately.

Fig relish

On holiday in southwest France one summer, and having just eaten an enormous Gallic lunch at the local restaurant, Guy ordered the cheese plate to finish his meal. When it arrived it had in its middle a large dollop of fig conserve with a cinnamon quill sticking out of it. Not only did the relish look spectacular, it tasted so good that he ordered the whole cheese plate a second time just so that he could enjoy more of the relish. This is our tribute to that delectable relish – and it goes perfectly with goat's cheese.

Makes 4–6 jars

1kg (2lb 4oz) dried figs, roughly chopped

450ml (16fl oz or 2 cups) hot water

450ml (16fl oz or 2 cups) cider vinegar

2 tsp black peppercorns

4 tsp whole allspice berries

2 tbsp whole cloves

1 cinnamon quill

1 tsp fresh red chilli, deseeded and finely chopped

400g (14oz or 2 cups) muscovado sugar

100g (3½oz or ½ cup) raw cane sugar

1. Put the chopped figs in a heatproof bowl and add the hot water. Leave to soak for an hour.

2. Meanwhile, make the spiced vinegar by putting the vinegar, peppercorns, allspice, cloves and cinnamon into a large saucepan. Bring to the boil before immediately removing from the heat and allowing to cool and infuse.

3. When cool, remove the spices with a slotted spoon. Add the figs and their juice to the pan and bring to the boil. Stir in the chilli, then add the sugars and bring back to the boil, stirring continuously to ensure that they have entirely dissolved.

4. Boil for about 20–30 minutes until the correct consistency is reached. Test by running a spoon along the bottom of the pan – if the channel you make doesn't fill immediately, the relish is ready. Spoon into sterilised jars and seal immediately.

Caramelised red onion relish

As you might expect from an onion that is most often eaten raw, red onions are milder than their white relations and consequently need a good belt of vinegar, which gives this relish a good piquancy. The added vinegar creates a product that is looser in texture and less sweet than our onion marmalade. It's really great in a steak sandwich or in a cheese quiche. Red onions lose their vibrant colour when cooked, so we use muscovado sugar to give it some depth of colour.

Makes 4–6 jars

2.5kg (5lb 8oz) or approximately 15 red onions, peeled and sliced

125g (4½oz or ⅔ cup) raw cane sugar

375g (13oz or generous 1¾ cups) muscovado sugar

500ml (18fl oz or 2¼ cups) cider vinegar

50ml (2fl oz or scant ¼ cup) balsamic vinegar

1½ tsp sea salt

Pinch of freshly ground black pepper

1. Put the sliced onions in a large saucepan. Put the pan on a low heat and gently sweat the onions (without adding any oil which would make the onions too greasy) for about an hour, or until they are soft and translucent. This is to remove as much liquid as possible.

2. Add the raw cane sugar and stir for another 10–15 minutes, being careful not to let the sugar catch on the bottom of the pan. The onion slices will start to caramelise.

3. Add the muscovado sugar and both vinegars and continue stirring while bringing to the boil. Finally, add the salt and pepper and cook for about 10 minutes until thick and jammy.

4. Spoon into sterilised jars and seal immediately.

Roasted cherry tomato relish

Summer, and its lighter style of eating, showcases different meals that demand fresh, bold flavours to accompany them. The star in this line-up is undoubtedly the versatile, juicy tomato, but if you grow your own you will inevitably have a glut of them and there will be some that are less tasty. Roasting them concentrates their flavour and transforms a tasteless tomato into one bursting with summer sunshine. Our friends at The Tomato Stall on the Isle of Wight supply us with wonderfully sweet tomatoes to use in this relish.

Makes 4–6 jars

1.3kg (3lb) cherry tomatoes

125ml (4fl oz or ½ cup) olive oil

2.5g (½ tbsp) fresh thyme leaves, washed and chopped

Pinch of freshly ground black pepper

450ml (16fl oz or 2 cups) cider vinegar

1 medium onion, peeled and finely diced

5 cloves of garlic, peeled and crushed

2 tbsp tomato purée, concentrated

15g (½oz or 1 tbsp) sea salt

1 fresh red chilli, deseeded and chopped

½ tsp whole coriander seeds

½ tsp whole cumin seeds

300g (10½oz or 1½ cups) raw cane sugar

1. Preheat the oven to 200°C/400°F/gas mark 6.

2. Cut the tomatoes in half across their middle, then spread them out in a roasting tin, cut-side up. Drizzle the tomatoes with the oil, and sprinkle with the thyme and pepper. Roast for 30 minutes.

3. While the tomatoes are roasting, put half the vinegar, the onion and garlic into a large, heavy-bottomed preserving pan. Bring to a simmer for 5–10 minutes to soften the onion. Add the rest of the vinegar, the tomatoes, tomato purée, salt and spices and give a good stir to mix. Bring to the boil.

4. Add the sugar and stir well to ensure that it is completely dissolved. Bring back to the boil, then lower the heat and simmer for 15–20 minutes until the mixture reaches a nice, soft consistency.

5. Spoon into sterilised jars and seal immediately.

Beetroot & horseradish relish

Putting these two earthy-tasting root vegetables together is a marriage made in heaven. Horseradish, famed for its power, poke and bitterness, perfectly balances the sweetness of the beetroot. It borrows heritage from the quintessentially Jewish condiment chrain, which is considered an essential accompaniment to gefilte fish.

It makes life much easier if you chill the horseradish root in the fridge for an hour before peeling and grating, as this tames its feisty fumes. Julienned beetroot will be crunchier, whereas grated beetroot will relax on cooking and make a softer product.

Makes 4–6 jars

1kg (2lb 4oz) beetroot, skins and at least 2.5cm (1 inch) of stalk left on

600ml (20fl oz or 2½ cups) malt vinegar

575g (1lb 5oz or 3 large) Bramley apples, peeled, cored and finely diced

635g (1lb 6oz or scant 3¼ cups) raw cane sugar

1 tsp sea salt

10ml (2 tsp) lemon juice

300g (10½oz) fresh horseradish root

1. Blanch the beetroot by bringing a pan of water to the boil and adding the whole beetroot, then bringing back to the boil for 3–5 minutes, depending on size. Remove the beetroot and rinse under cold water to stop them cooking any further. When cool enough to handle, peel them and discard the skins. Using a sharp knife, top and tail the beetroot before either grating or julienning them into 2-mm (1/16-inch) sticks.

2. In a large, heavy-bottomed preserving pan, heat the vinegar until just simmering, add the apples and cook for 5 minutes, or until the apple is soft and pulpy. Add the beetroot, sugar, salt and lemon juice and bring to the boil, stirring frequently until the sugar is completely dissolved and the mixture thickens. Gently boil the mixture for about 20 minutes, or until you like the consistency. Remove from the heat and leave to cool in the pan.

3. While it is cooling, grate and then whizz the horseradish in a food processor for a couple of seconds until there are no large lumps. In order to preserve the power of the horseradish, the mixture in the pan must be completely cool before the horseradish is added. Add the horseradish to the pan and stir well.

4. Spoon into sterilised jars. In this recipe because the mixture is cold when you fill the jars, it is better to fill them quite full and perhaps put a disc of greaseproof paper on the top to keep the air off the surface of the relish. Once opened keep in the fridge and consume within three months to enjoy the horseradish at its full strength.

Sweetcorn relish

On a trip to Rhode Island to visit our American distributors we tasted a wonderful corn relish that was the inspiration for this product. Crunchy, golden corn that explodes when you eat it in a spicy sauce makes a superb accompaniment to homemade burgers. Better still, it doesn't require a big investment in time to make.

Makes 4–6 jars

450ml (16fl oz or 2 cups) cider vinegar

350g (12oz or 1¾ cups) raw cane sugar

1kg (2lb 4oz) sweetcorn kernels

300g (10½oz) or approximately 3 red peppers, diced to 5mm (¼ inch)

300g (10½oz) or approximately 3 green peppers, diced to 5mm (¼ inch)

1 medium onion, peeled and diced

250g (9oz or 2½ cups) celery, diced

2 tsp yellow mustard seeds

2 tbsp mustard powder

1 tsp celery seeds

25g (1½ tbsp) sea salt

1 fresh red chilli, deseeded and finely chopped

20g (¾oz or 2 tbsp) cornflour, mixed with a little water

1. Put the vinegar and sugar in a large, heavy-bottomed preserving pan and warm gently until the sugar has dissolved. Bring to the boil and add the vegetables. Stir well.

2. Add the mustard seeds, mustard powder, celery seeds, salt and chilli. Boil for 30 minutes, stirring regularly.

3. Stir the cornflour paste into the relish. Bring back to the boil and continue to boil until the desired consistency is reached. Spoon into sterilised jars and seal immediately.

Pickled onion relish

Even if you have a genuine love of pickled onions, there always seem
to be one or two lurking in the bottom of an unfinished jar in the
cupboard. After a larder spring clean we decided to experiment and
see if we could use them to make a relish. The result is awesome, even
if we do say so ourselves!

Makes 3–5 jars

400ml (14fl oz or 1¾ cups)
malt vinegar

1 tsp (approximately 18)
allspice berries

1 tsp black peppercorns

1kg (2lb 4oz) pickled onions

250g (9oz or 1¼ cups)
raw cane sugar

75g (2¾oz or ⅓ cup + 2 tsp)
muscovado sugar

1 fresh red chilli, deseeded and
finely diced

1 tsp brown mustard seeds

1. Make a spiced vinegar by putting the vinegar in a small pan with the
allspice and peppercorns and heating to just boiling before removing from
the heat. Allow to cool and infuse for up to an hour.

2. Meanwhile, whizz the pickled onions for a few seconds in a food processor
or with a stick blender so that they are quite finely chopped.

3. When the vinegar is cool, put both it and the onions in a large, heavy-
bottomed preserving pan and bring to the boil.

4. Stir in the raw cane sugar. When it has dissolved add the muscovado
sugar, stirring to make sure it dissolves completely. Add the chilli and
mustard seeds.

5. Bring back to the boil and continue boiling until the desired consistency
is reached. Spoon into sterilised jars and seal immediately.

Bloody Mary relish

This started life as one of our limited-edition seasonal products that use only British produce, so we had to source a British vodka. It's a great relish, which, like its namesake, is a real pick-me-up, with a tasty zing and moreish piquancy all of its own.

Makes 4–6 jars

For the spiced vinegar

700ml (24fl oz or 3 cups) cider vinegar

1 heaped tsp black peppercorns

2 tsp allspice berries

2 tsp coriander seeds

1 heaped tsp fenugreek seeds

3 dried bird's-eye chillies or ½ tsp dried crushed chillies

For the relish

1 medium onion, peeled and finely chopped

500g (1lb 2oz or 5 cups) celery, finely diced

800g (1lb 12oz) or approximately 10 tomatoes, chopped into 1-cm (½-inch) pieces

230g (8oz) or approximately 1½ Bramley apples, peeled, cored and chopped into 1-cm (½-inch) pieces

1 tsp sea salt

Pinch of curry powder

200g (7oz or 1¼ cups) sultanas, roughly chopped

150g (5½oz or ¾ cup) raw cane sugar

150g (5½oz or ¾ cup) muscovado sugar

20ml (4 tsp) vodka (optional)

1. Make the spiced vinegar by putting the vinegar, peppercorns, allspice, coriander and fenugreek seeds and chillies into a pan, bring to the boil, then remove immediately from the heat. Allow to cool and infuse for 30 minutes while you prepare the rest of the ingredients.

2. When the vinegar has cooled remove the spices using a slotted spoon and pour the liquid into a large, heavy-bottomed preserving pan. Add the onion and celery and bring to the boil, then lower the heat and simmer for 5 minutes. Add the tomatoes and apples and bring back to the boil for a couple of minutes.

3. Add the salt, curry powder and sultanas and mix well before gradually adding the sugars. Stir constantly to ensure that the sugars dissolve completely, then bring back to the boil and cook until the desired consistency is reached. Test by running a spoon along the bottom of the pan – if the channel you make doesn't fill immediately, the relish is ready.

4. Remove from the heat and stir in the vodka, if using. Spoon into sterilised jars and seal immediately.

Pickled walnut relish

When you think about pickled walnuts (which Guy says he does frequently), they can often be rather intimidating. But these mysterious dark jewels can be transformed into a piquant relish that's perfect for bringing out the best in a good, strong Cheddar or a thick slice of cold gammon. So if you've been given a jar or two of pickled walnuts for Christmas and are at a loss as to how to use them, try this recipe and enjoy using the result all year round.

Makes 3–5 jars

For the spiced vinegar

400ml (14fl oz or 1¾ cups) malt vinegar

1 tsp (approximately 18) allspice berries

1 tsp black peppercorns

approximately 12 whole dried bird's-eye chillies

For the relish

1 medium onion, peeled and finely chopped

1 medium Bramley apple, peeled, cored and finely chopped

600g (1lb 5oz) pickled walnuts, drained and roughly chopped

50g (1¾oz or scant ⅓cup) dried seedless dates, roughly chopped

335g (11½oz or 1½ cups + 2 tbsp) raw cane sugar

1. Make the spiced vinegar by putting the vinegar in a pan with the allspice, peppercorns and dried chillies, Bring to the boil, then remove from the heat immediately and allow to cool and infuse for between 20 and 60 minutes. When cool remove the spices with a slotted spoon.

2. Put the vinegar in a large, heavy-bottomed preserving pan, add the onion and apples and bring to the boil. Boil for a couple of minutes, then add the walnuts and dates. Give the mixture a good stir and allow to bubble for a further couple of minutes.

3. Add the sugar and stir well to ensure that the sugar is completely dissolved. Bring back to a rolling boil for 6–10 minutes, or until the desired consistency is reached. Test by running a spoon along the bottom of the pan – if the channel you make doesn't fill immediately, the relish is ready.

4. Remove from the heat, spoon into sterilised jars and seal immediately.

Tomato & pepper salsa

A warm, balmy summer evening, a picnic rug on the river bank, dragonflies darting over the water and a glass of crisp white wine with a bag of crisps made us wonder why on earth we hadn't made a good old-fashioned dip for crisps. So now we have.

If this salsa isn't hot enough for you, you can always experiment and substitute habanero chillies for the red chillies. Habanero chillies can be up to a hundred times as hot as jalapeño chillies, according to the Scoville scale (see page 10). For a very different flavour and to give your salsa a deep, smoky touch, try using chipotle chillies, which are jalapeño peppers that have been smoked.

Makes 4–7 jars

400ml (14fl oz or 1¾ cups) cider vinegar

95ml (3fl oz or ⅓ cup) sunflower oil

275g (9½oz or 1⅓ cups) raw cane sugar

2 large onions, peeled and diced

3 red peppers, deseeded and diced

4–5 fresh red chillies, deseeded and chopped

25g (1oz or 1½ tbsp) sea salt

190g (6½oz) tomatoes, chopped into 1-cm (½-inch) pieces

175g (6oz or ¾ cup) tomato purée (see page 142)

1. Heat the vinegar, oil and sugar in a large, heavy-bottomed preserving pan. Add the onions, peppers and chillies and bring to the boil.

2. Add the salt, tomatoes and tomato purée. Bring back to the boil and boil for 5–10 minutes, or until you like the look of the consistency.

3. Remove from the heat, spoon into sterilised jars and seal immediately. The salsa will keep for three months in the fridge.

Salsa verde

Literally meaning 'green sauce', there are as many recipes for this cold sauce as there are villages in Italy. With its fusion of herbs and flavours, it's a deliciously refreshing and punchy mixture that is ideal for transforming simple into spectacular. Frequently served with squid or fish, it is equally delightful on grilled meats or a green salad.

You can make the salsa in several ways; either use a mini food processor, which is the method we've described here, or else a pestle and mortar. Chopping the herbs by hand will create a coarser paste.

Makes 1–2 jars

4 tsp capers, drained

2 cloves of garlic, peeled

6 fillets salted anchovies

30ml (2 tbsp) red wine vinegar

60ml (4 tbsp) olive oil

1 small handful
fresh parsley, washed

1 small handful
fresh basil leaves, washed

1 rounded tsp
fresh mint leaves, washed

¼ tsp sea salt

1½ tbsp Dijon mustard

1. Add the capers, garlic, anchovies and vinegar to a food processor bowl and pulse. Then add the rest of the ingredients and pulse to the consistency of a paste rather than a purée.

2. You can either use immediately or keep in a covered bowl for up to a week in the fridge.

3. The salsa will keep for up to two months in the fridge if you do the following: spoon the salsa into a jar, tap the jar on a surface to remove any air bubbles and pour a layer of olive oil on top of the salsa to form a seal. Seal immediately. Stir before using.

Roasted mixed pepper relish

We were invited to take our products to the largest exposition of artisan foods in Europe, Salone del Gusto, an event that took us by surprise not only for its sheer size but also because of the Italians' enthusiasm for our products. It was there that we were introduced to the Italian version of tracklements in the form of roasted mixed peppers served with salami and prosciutto as an antipasto. We enjoyed it so much that we decided to make our own.

Makes 4–6 jars

3 yellow peppers, quartered and deseeded

5 red peppers, quartered and deseeded

130ml (4½fl oz or generous ½ cup) olive oil

5 tomatoes

2 medium onions, peeled and finely sliced

180g (6oz or scant 1 cup) raw cane sugar

15g (½oz or 1 tbsp) sea salt

250ml (9fl oz or 1 cup + 2 tbsp) cider vinegar

100ml (3½fl oz or scant ½ cup) balsamic vinegar

6–8 cloves of garlic, peeled and crushed

2 fresh red chillies, deseeded and finely diced

100g (3½oz or a generous ½ cup) tomato purée concentrate

1. Place the peppers skin-side up on a baking sheet, drizzle with a little of the oil and put under a hot grill until the skins have completely blistered and turned black: this takes about 5–10 minutes. Remove from under the grill and cover with clingfilm, or put in a sealed plastic bag and leave to cool. This makes the skins really easy to peel off.

2. While the peppers are cooling prepare the tomatoes. Using a sharp knife, make an cross incision in the skin on the bottom of the tomatoes, then put them in a bowl and cover with boiling water for 1–2 minutes, or until their skins split and come off easily. Cut into chunks. Then once the peppers are cool enough, skin them and cut into strips about 5mm (¼ inch) wide.

3. Place the onions in a large, heavy-bottomed preserving pan with 30ml (2 tablespoons) olive oil. Put the pan on a medium heat and gently sweat the onions for 15–20 minutes, or until they are soft and translucent. This removes their liquid.

4. Add the raw cane sugar and stir over the heat for another 10–15 minutes, being careful not to let the sugar catch on the bottom of the pan. The onions will caramelise and turn a golden colour.

5. Add the salt and the vinegars and bring to the boil, lower the heat and simmer for 5 minutes, then add the tomatoes, garlic and chillies and simmer for a further 3–5 minutes. Add the peppers and simmer for 5 minutes. Finally, add the tomato purée and the rest of the olive oil and stir well. Remove from the heat. Spoon into sterilised jars and seal immediately.

Balsamic salsa

Ably demonstrating how versatile and eclectic these Mediterranean salsas are, this one came about one evening while looking for something to liven up a bowl of pasta. Rich and unctuous balsamic vinegar cooked with peppers and tomatoes made the perfect summer evening supper.

Makes 4–7 jars

200ml (7fl oz or scant 1 cup) cider vinegar

250ml (9fl oz or 1 cup + 2 tbsp) balsamic vinegar

95ml (3fl oz or ⅓ cup) sunflower oil

2 large onions, peeled and diced

2 red peppers, deseeded and diced

2 green peppers, deseeded and diced

25g (1oz or 1½ tbsp) sea salt

2 fresh red chillies, deseeded and finely chopped

2 fresh green chillies, deseeded and finely chopped

2 cloves of garlic, peeled and crushed

275g (9¾oz or 1⅓ cups) raw cane sugar

a small handful of fresh rosemary leaves, chopped

190g (6½oz) tomatoes, chopped into 1-cm (½-inch) pieces

175g (6oz or ¾ cup) tomato purée concentrate

1. Heat the vinegars and the oil in a large, heavy-bottomed preserving pan, then add the onions and simmer for 5–10 minutes to soften.

2. Add the peppers and bring to a vigorous boil. Add the salt, chillies and garlic and boil for another couple of minutes before adding the sugar.

3. Stir well to ensure the sugar is completely dissolved. Bring to the boil. Add the rosemary, tomatoes and tomato purée and continue to cook until the desired consistency is reached. Test by running a spoon along the bottom of the pan – if the channel you make doesn't fill immediately, the relish is ready.

4. Spoon into sterilised jars and seal immediately.

Caponata

The Sicilian equivalent of British chutney, *caponata* encapsulates the history of preserving. It was originally made to be taken on long voyages by Sicilian sailors, allowing them to enjoy the taste of home. It features Mediterranean vegetables cooked in sweetened vinegar to give it its characteristic sweet-sour balance. Now incredibly popular all over Italy, it is eaten warm as a side dish, cold as antipasti with cold cuts or spooned onto pasta to make a sauce. We have been loaned this recipe by our friend and aficionada in all things Italian Angela Hartnett, from her cookbook *Cucina*.

Makes 2–4 jars

2 large aubergines, cut into 2-cm (¾-inch) cubes

Sea salt

4 plum tomatoes

120ml (4fl oz or ½ cup) olive oil

1 medium onion peeled and chopped into 2-cm (¾-inch) dice

2 celery sticks, sliced

1 red pepper, deseeded and chopped into 2-cm (¾-inch) dice

2 large courgettes, sliced into 1-cm (½-inch) rounds

50g (1¾oz) pine nuts, lightly toasted

50g (1¾oz) capers, rinsed

50g (1¾oz) green olives, pitted and roughly chopped

Salt and freshly ground black pepper

1 handful fresh basil leaves, roughly chopped

1. Preheat the oven to 160°C/325°F/gas mark 3.

2. Put the aubergines in a colander and sprinkle with salt. Set aside for 10–15 minutes to release their juices.

3. Meanwhile, prepare the tomatoes. Make a little incision with a sharp knife in the top of each one. Bring a pan of salted water to the boil and blanch the tomatoes in it for 10 seconds. Drain and transfer immediately to a bowl of cold water. Peel, quarter and deseed the tomatoes, then cut each quarter into three.

4. Pat the aubergine cubes dry. Heat 6 tablespoons of the olive oil in a frying pan over a fairly high heat – it should be hot enough so that the aubergine sizzles but doesn't burn; if the oil is too cool the aubergine will just soak it up. Fry the aubergine cubes in batches until golden brown, transferring the cooked pieces to a colander to get rid of any excess oil.

5. Return the empty pan to the heat and add the remaining olive oil. Add the onion and celery and sauté for 3–4 minutes, or until golden brown. Add the red pepper and cook for 3 minutes, followed by the courgettes for a further 2–3 minutes. Then add the aubergines and tomatoes and cook for a further 2–3 minutes, stirring constantly. All the vegetables should be tender and heated through but not too soft.

6. Finally, stir in the pine nuts, capers and olives, season well and add the basil. You can eat this immediately, or transfer to sterilised jars and seal immediately. It will keep in the fridge for up to three days.

SAUCES

'The one infallible sign of civilisation and enlightenment. A people
with no sauces has one thousand vices; a people with one sauce
has only 999. For every sauce invented and accepted, a vice is
renounced and forgiven.'
Ambrose Bierce, *The Devil's Dictionary*, 1911

The word 'sauce' covers all number and manner of culinary adventures that seem
to have little or no relation to each other, except for their usefulness in cooking
and eating, and perhaps their consistency. Some are poured – béchamel, for
example. Some are served on the side, such as bread sauce, and some are the focus
of the dish, like Bolognese sauce for pasta. Nor is the word limited only to savoury
accompaniments; a sticky toffee pudding without a hot fudge sauce is unthinkable.
However, the particular bottled sauces featured in this chapter form their own
exclusive sub-category.

I'm not sure that Alice B. Toklas meant for us to take it literally when she said
'What is sauce for the goose may be sauce for the gander but is not necessarily sauce
for the chicken, the duck, the turkey or the guinea hen.' But how right she was. Each
and every meat has a specific sauce that has been made to accompany it. Think mint
sauce for lamb, apple sauce for pork, dill sauce for salmon and plum sauce for duck.
Rarely do they seem to exceed the limit of this use, or cross over from one meat to
another. Of course, as with every rule there are a few exceptions.

These 'perfect pairing' sauces probably grew out of a surfeit, not of their own
ingredients but of the meat that they accompany. After all, when a bullock, lamb or
pig was slaughtered for the table, there was a lot of meat to eat and a limited time
in which to eat it, and culinary enjoyment demanded different ways of eating it and
different sauces to accompany it. On being presented with a large quantity of meat,
the cook would have looked around to see what herbs, fruit or vegetables nature had
provided at the same time, and chosen those as the basis of the sauce to accompany

it. The family pig was slaughtered in the autumn at the same time that orchards overflowed with ripe, juicy apples. Garden mint runs rampant in spring, when lamb becomes available. Cattle were killed in the autumn, when the easily accessible horseradish roots are at their strongest, putting all the power and flavour into the root rather than using energy in flowering. Possibly the horseradish was the only green thing left in the field after the cattle had grazed it as cows won't eat the strong-tasting plants.

Perhaps as another part of Nature's great plan, the ingredients we use in these sauces also have additional benefits other than availability; their slight acidity perfectly complements the fattiness of meat and brings out its sweet taste.

These meat-and-sauce pairings have been tried and tested down the years, and roast meats and the flavours that accompany them form a timeless institution. As with all things, it is the little things that make all the difference, and never is this truer than with roast meats and their tracklements. Imagine roast lamb without the piquant sharpness of mint, roast pork without the fruity burst of apple sauce or roast beef without lively, reviving horseradish on the side.

Making sauces

Although the best sauce accompaniments are freshly made and brought to the table, that is not always practical or possible. Therefore it is the challenge of the sauce-maker to capture the freshness of the ingredient and prepare it to be stored for ease and convenience of use.

A freshly made mint sauce will always taste different from a preserved one, but we believe they both have their places at the table and that there is no need (or indeed excuse) for a flat, sharp or grey mint sauce from a jar.

The variety and individuality of sauces means that ingredients vary, but the skill lies in the preserver's art of balancing sugar and vinegar to augment not only the vibrancy of the original ingredient but also its integrity. More than any other accompaniments, sauces fulfil our requirement for bitter, sweet, sour and salt: their own version of umami.

Unlike pickles, chutneys and jellies, there are no hard-and-fast rules when it comes to making sauces; each relies on its own particular method, and the storage time will vary, too.

Fresh horseradish sauce

Horseradish has been treasured by gourmands, medicine men and cooks throughout history. There are references to its use dating back to 1500 BC. This powerful, universally available root has been prized for its bitter taste as well as its medicinal qualities, although in all that time a consensus on why it's called 'horseradish' has never been satisfactorily reached. The most likely explanation seems to be that horseradish grew by the sea in parts of Europe, and was therefore given the German name *Meerrettich*, meaning 'sea radish', which the English misheard as 'mare', the name for a female horse.

Horseradish is white to cream-coloured when fresh, turning darker beige as it ages. Although still edible, this shows that the root is losing its flavour and power. It is best to chill the root for an hour or so in the fridge before peeling and grating it; your eyes and tear ducts will thank you for it.

Makes 4–6 small jars

500g (1lb 2oz) fresh horseradish root, peeled and freshly grated

80ml (3fl oz or ⅓ cup) spirit or distilled malt vinegar

1 tsp lemon juice

115ml (4fl oz or ½ cup) single cream

1 tsp sea salt

10g (¼oz or 2 tsp) raw cane sugar

1 tsp mustard powder

250ml (9fl oz or 1 cup + 2 tbsp) sunflower oil

1. Mix the grated horseradish with the vinegar and lemon juice and blitz them in a food processor until you have a coarse consistency. You are not aiming for a purée.

2. Add the cream, salt, sugar, mustard powder and oil and give it another 15-second whizz. If the sauce is too thick you can add a little more cream.

3. Put into sterilised jars and seal immediately. The sauce will keep for up to three months in the fridge.

Dill sauce

Every Scandinavian family has its own recipe for dill sauce, and Tracklements' founders, the Tullbergs, are no exception. One of Guy's signature dishes is gravadlax: salmon cured with salt, pepper and sugar. Gravadlax was originally made to last the whole winter, and by the end of the preserving process it packed some wallop. Consequently it needed a sauce that would also pack a punch – which this one does admirably!

Makes 4–6 small jars

185g (6½oz) Dijon mustard

185g (6½oz) wholegrain mustard

110ml (4fl oz or ½ cup) honey

75g (2¾oz or ⅓ cup + 2 tsp) raw cane sugar

2 tsp sea salt

220ml (8fl oz or 1 cup) sunflower oil

a large handful of fresh dill, washed and finely chopped

1. Put the mustards, honey, sugar and salt into a food processor and whizz for 15 seconds.

2. With the processor running on the slowest setting, gradually add the oil until the mixture emulsifies.

3. Transfer into a bowl and fold the finely chopped dill in by hand until it's evenly distributed.

4. You can either use immediately or keep in a covered bowl in the fridge for up to a week. Transferred to sterilised jars and sealed, the sauce will keep in the fridge for six months.

Apple & cider brandy sauce

One of nature's great pairings is pork and apple sauce. Pigs have long been used to rootle around orchards, keeping the soil in good condition and the pests at bay while providing invaluable fertiliser for apple trees. The trees in turn gave up their bountiful fruit just as the animals were slaughtered for the winter, so it made absolute sense for the cook to use them to enhance this delicious meat. This sauce is simple and quick to make.

Makes 3–5 jars

150ml (5fl oz or ⅔cup) cider vinegar

30ml (1fl oz or 2 tbsp) lemon juice

5 Bramley apples, peeled, cored and chopped into 2-cm (¾-inch) pieces

200g (7oz or 1 cup) raw cane sugar

Pinch of nutmeg

Pinch of cinnamon

15ml (1 tbsp) cider brandy or dry cider

1. Put the vinegar, lemon juice and apples in a large, heavy-bottomed preserving pan. Place on a low heat until the apple pieces begin to break up.

2. Stir in the sugar, spices and cider brandy or cider and continue to stir until the sugar is completely dissolved and you have reached the desired consistency. Test for a good consistency by drawing the spoon along the bottom of the pan; if the channel formed doesn't fill in immediately, the sauce is ready.

3. Spoon into sterilised jars and seal immediately. This will keep for up to three months in the fridge.

Mint sauce

Mint was grown and used by both the Greeks and Romans and has remained popular ever since for its sweet, refreshing taste as well as its beneficial digestive qualities. In his 16th-century work, *The Herball, or Generall Historie of Plantes*, John Gerard wrote, 'The smell of mint does stir up the minde and the taste to a greedy desire of meat' – a sentiment with which we wholeheartedly agree, particularly with respect to lamb.

Most cuisines around the world recognise the benefit of a sharply flavoured sauce to cut through the rich, strong taste of lamb. There are over a hundred varieties of this wonderful herb and the taste of your sauce will be affected by the type of mint you choose. Young leaves are better as they are softer and more tender.

Makes 2–4 small jars

100g (3½oz) fresh mint leaves

1 tsp sea salt

310ml (11fl oz or 1⅓ cups) cider vinegar

350g (12oz or 1¾ cups) raw cane sugar

10ml (2 tsp) lemon juice

1. Strip the mint leaves from the stalks and discard the stalks. It takes a while to chop the mint by hand, especially as it needs to be a really fine chop; the pieces should be no more than 3mm (⅛ inch) in diameter. An alternative is to blitz them with a stick blender or in a mini food processor. After chopping sprinkle the salt over the mint, mix well and then set aside.

2. Put the vinegar into a pan and heat gently. Add half the sugar and the lemon juice and stir until the sugar has completely dissolved. Add the remaining sugar, stirring continuously. When the sugar has dissolved, bring the mixture to the boil and boil for about 2–3 minutes until a good, syrupy texture is achieved. Remove from the heat and stir in the chopped mint and salt mixture.

3. Leave the sauce to cool for 5 minutes, then put into sterilised jars and seal immediately.

Cranberry & orange sauce with port

We think of cranberries as American, and indeed they are, along with other native North American berries such as the blueberry and the Concord grape. The name comes from 'craneberry', because when European settlers first arrived in North America, the plant's small, pink spring flowers reminded them of the head and bill of the sandhill crane. Native Americans have eaten cranberries for centuries, and early whalers and sailors used them to prevent scurvy. They have been cultivated in North America since the early 19th century, and cranberry sauce is now firmly entrenched as part of the American Thanksgiving tradition.

Makes 8–12 jars

500ml (18fl oz or 2¼ cups) cider vinegar

100ml (3½fl oz or scant ½ cup) lemon juice

2kg (4lb 8oz or 10 cups) raw cane sugar

1kg (2lb 4oz) fresh cranberries, rinsed and roughly chopped

grated zest of 2½ oranges

70ml (2½fl oz or scant ⅓ cup) port

1. Put the vinegar, lemon juice and half the sugar into a large, heavy-bottomed preserving pan. Bring to the boil, stirring well to ensure that the sugar has completely dissolved.

2. Add the chopped cranberries and orange zest, and stir gently so that the fruit isn't 'mushed'. Bring back to the boil. Add the remaining sugar, again stirring continuously until it has dissolved.

3. Continue boiling for about 10 minutes until the mixture thickens. Remove from the heat and leave to cool for 5–10 minutes, or until the fruit stops rising to the surface. Stir in the port. Spoon the sauce into sterilised jars and seal immediately.

Cumberland sauce

This deliciously fruity, rich sauce for duck and game originated in Germany, where there has always been a well-established custom of eating fruity sauces with meat. It gained its name of Cumberland thanks to its popularity with the King of Hanover, who was also known as the Duke of Cumberland and brother of George IV. It was his fondness for this sauce that brought it to the attention and ministrations of English cooks – and we have never looked back.

Makes 2–4 jars
½ tsp yellow mustard seeds
50ml (2fl oz or scant ¼ cup) port
Pinch of ground ginger
Small pinch of chilli powder
1kg (2lb 4oz) redcurrant jelly
15ml (½fl oz or 1 tbsp) orange juice
15ml (½fl oz or 1 tbsp) lemon juice
grated zest of 1 orange

1. Grind the mustard seeds until they form a coarse grind. Add them to the port along with the ginger and chilli powder, and leave in a warm place to infuse for 30 minutes.

2. Put the redcurrant jelly into a large, heavy-bottomed preserving pan and heat gently until liquid. Add the orange juice, the lemon juice and orange zest and bring just to the boil before removing from the heat.

3. Stir in the port mixture and leave to cool for 5 minutes. Stir again and pour immediately into sterilised jars – this makes sure the port is evenly distributed through the sauce. Seal immediately.

Plum sauce

The sharp-flavoured plum has long been regarded as the best accompaniment to fatty meats like duck or pork belly. Ideally, only plums that are too tart for eating raw should be used for this sauce, so if you have a tree in the garden dripping with sour fruit, use it to make this wonderfully fruity condiment. Smooth and glossy, it is an ideal complement for gamey meats.

Makes 6–8 bottles

1 medium onion, peeled and finely chopped

500ml (18fl oz or 2¼ cups) cider vinegar

5 star anise

1kg (2lb 4oz) plums

1 tsp sea salt

50ml (2fl oz or scant ¼ cup) soy sauce

500g (1lb 2oz or 2½ cups) raw cane sugar

500g (1lb 2oz or 2½ cups) muscovado sugar

1. Put the onion into a large, heavy-bottomed preserving pan with the vinegar and bring to the boil. Lower the heat and simmer for 5 minutes to soften the onion.

2. Place the star anise into a piece of muslin to form a spice bag (see page 17) and tie it on to the side of the pan, low enough that it will covered by the other ingredients.

3. Add the plums, bring back to the boil, lower the heat and continue to simmer for a further 10 minutes, or until the fruit is really soft.

4. Add the salt, soy sauce and the sugars, stirring really well to ensure that the sugars have completely dissolved.

5. When the mixture is soft and mushy, pour it into a sieve set over a bowl and press through, using the back of a wooden spoon. Alternatively, pass the mixture through a mouli to extract all the purée while leaving any stones and skin behind.

6. Rinse out the pan and pour the purée back in. Bring back to the boil and boil until you are happy that you have a pourable consistency. Spoon into sterilised jars and seal immediately.

Steak sauce

Our good friends Sophie and Rupert from Sophie's Steakhouse in London wanted a really great pouring sauce to complement their fantastic British dry-aged steaks, which is how this fruity, sticky sauce was born. Our thanks to them for allowing us to publish it here for your enjoyment.

Makes 2–4 bottles

330ml (11fl oz or 1⅓ cups) malt vinegar

40ml (1½fl oz or 8 tsp) soy sauce

80ml (3fl oz or ⅓ cup) water

400g (14oz or 2 cups) raw cane sugar

600g (1lb 5oz) tomato purée (see page 142)

70ml (2½fl oz or scant ⅓ cup) Worcestershire sauce

40g (1½oz) fresh horseradish root, peeled and grated

1. Put the vinegar, soy sauce and water into a large, heavy-bottomed preserving pan and place over a medium heat. Add the sugar and stir until it has completely dissolved, then bring to the boil. Continue boiling for 2 minutes.

2. Add the tomato purée and stir well. Continue to boil for about 10–20 minutes until the desired consistency is reached. Remove from the heat and stir in the Worcestershire sauce. Leave to cool.

3. Meanwhile, place the grated horseradish in a food processor and blitz until it is finely ground and there are no large lumps. You can also use a stick blender.

4. Stir the horseradish into the cooling sauce. Spoon into sterilised jars and seal immediately.

Tartare sauce

This piquant sauce is said to get its name from a 13th-century French word for the Tatars – the Turkish Mongolian people who were renowned for their fierceness. In essence it is mayonnaise with attitude and a tangy assertiveness that perfectly balances soft, oily fish such as fillets of mackerel. We prefer to use curly parsley leaves in this recipe as it allows the sauce something to 'grip' onto but in terms of taste it doesn't matter whether you use curly or flat-leaf parsley.

Makes 2–4 small jars

2 heaped tsp strong English mustard

50ml (2fl oz or scant ¼ cup) sunflower oil

15g (½oz or 1 tbsp) raw cane sugar

3.5g (½ tsp) sea salt

1 small clove garlic, peeled and crushed

75g (2¾oz) silverskin onions, drained

25g (1oz) capers, drained

100g (3½oz) gherkins, drained

325g (11½oz) mayonnaise

a small handful of fresh parsley leaves, very finely chopped

1. Put the mustard, oil, sugar, salt, crushed garlic, onions, capers and gherkins into a food processor and whizz for 5–10 seconds until the mixture has a chunky consistency.

2. Put the mayonnaise and parsley into a bowl and carefully fold in the mustard mixture.

3. Spoon the sauce into sterilised jars and seal immediately. This will keep for up to three months in the fridge.

Hot, sweet chilli sauce

In specialist Chinese and Thai grocers there are row upon row of bottled chilli sauces. These fiery-hot sauces are used for dipping everything into, from wontons to meat patties. Our version of this thin dipping sauce gives an intense burst of heat to whatever is dipped into it.

Makes 1–2 bottles

250ml (9fl oz or 1 cup + 2 tbsp) water

1tsp dried chillies (whole bird's-eye chillies if possible)

4 fresh red chillies, deseeded and roughly chopped

2 cloves of garlic, peeled and chopped

2 tsp sea salt

250g (9oz or 1¼ cups) raw cane sugar

100ml (3½fl oz or scant ½ cup) spirit or distilled malt vinegar

1. Warm the water in a small pan and add the dried chillies. Bring to the boil, then add the fresh chillies and garlic and return to the boil. Add the salt, sugar and the vinegar and bring back to the boil.

2. Remove immediately from the heat and, using a stick blender, pulse until there are no pieces of chilli left.

3. Return the pan to the heat, bring back to the boil and boil vigorously for 10 minutes, stirring frequently.

4. Remove from the heat, pour into sterilised bottles and seal immediately.

Mayonnaise

The traditional way of making mayo is to use a hand whisk as this gives greater control. However, we think it's easier on the wrist to let a blender take the strain. All the ingredients should be at room temperature before you start and blended in the correct order.

Makes 2 large jars

2 medium egg yolks (reserve the egg whites)

½ tsp sea salt

1 tsp Dijon mustard

190ml (6½fl oz or scant 1 cup) sunflower oil

1 tsp cider vinegar

2 tsp lemon juice

1. Add the egg yolks, salt and mustard to a blender or beat with a whisk until the yolks begin to thicken slightly. If you prefer a lighter mayo, add one of the reserved egg whites to the egg yolks.

2. Begin adding the oil, a little at a time and blend or whisk each addition thoroughly until the mixture begins to emulsify. Once it starts to emulsify you can add the oil more quickly.

3. Continue to add the remaining oil and then add the vinegar and lemon juice until the mayonnaise is thick and unctuous. This is also the time to add any other variations.

4. Should your mayonnaise curdle or fail to thicken, don't worry. Either add a little of the reserved egg white and beat again, or start again with another beaten, thickened egg yolk and gradually add the mixture to the egg.

5. Transfer to a sterilised jar, cover and store in the fridge for up to one week.

Variations

If you prefer a garlicky mayo add ½ clove, peeled and crushed, to step 3. For a good mustardy mayo add a second teaspoon of Dijon mustard, also to step 3.

Béarnaise sauce

There are some moments when only a comforting steak and chips will do the business, and surely the best accompaniment on these occasions is a smooth, creamy béarnaise sauce. The lightness of this French sauce belies its ingredients but it is devilishly delicious.

Makes 1 small jar

50ml (2fl oz or scant ¼ cup) white wine vinegar

50ml (2fl oz or scant ¼ cup) water

1 shallot, peeled and very finely chopped

8 black peppercorns

200g (7oz or scant 1 cup) unsalted butter

6 medium egg yolks

a small handful of fresh tarragon leaves, washed and finely chopped

Pinch of freshly ground black pepper

Pinch of sea salt

1. Put the vinegar, water, shallot and peppercorns into a small pan over a low–medium heat and reduce it down until half the liquid remains (this should take about 3–5 minutes).

2. Remove the pan from the heat. Take out the shallot and peppercorns with a slotted spoon and set the vinegar to one side to cool completely. There should now be about 50ml (2fl oz or scant ¼ cup) of liquid.

3. Heat the butter gently until it is completely melted. Set aside to cool to a tepid temperature.

4. Add the reduction and the egg yolks to a blender and pulse for 5–10 seconds on the slowest setting.

5. Keeping the blender on the slowest speed, very, very slowly add the melted butter and continue to whizz until the desired thickness is reached – about 30 seconds.

6. Pour the sauce into a bowl and stir in the fresh tarragon leaves. Add salt and pepper to taste. Serve at room temperature.

7. You can either use the sauce immediately or it will keep for up to a week in the fridge in a sterilised jar.

Hollandaise sauce

Speed and organisation are required when making hollandaise. It's important to combine all the ingredients at the right time at the correct temperature. This is delicious served with lightly steamed asparagus or hot or cold poached salmon.

Makes 2 jars

2 tsp cider vinegar

2 tsp lemon juice

200g (7oz or scant 1 cup) unsalted butter

4 medium egg yolks

½ tsp sea salt

1. Gently heat the vinegar and lemon juice and keep warm.

2. Melt the butter in a saucepan, stirring all the time, until it begins to foam – try not to let it boil.

3. Add the egg yolks and salt to a blender and whizz for a few seconds. With the blade still running add the hot vinegar and lemon juice mixture.

4. Finally, slowly add the hot butter, a little at a time as the mixture begins to thicken and then switch off the blender. It should be thick enough to coat the end of your finger – or stick to the end of an asparagus spear!

5. If it fails to thicken add a tablespoon of hot water to the mixture with the blade running.

6. You can either use the sauce immediately or it will keep for up to a week in the fridge in a sterilised jar.

7. Hollandaise sauce should be served warm, so just before serving, warm a ramekin dish for a minute or so in the microwave and then spoon the sauce into the hot dish.

Pesto

Every year we have a Tracklements summer party for all our staff, and at one of these events we were shown how to make fresh pasta with pesto by an expert. We were then put into teams and challenged to make our own lunch. The pasta shapes may have been eclectic but the pesto was delicious and we were all surprised by how easy it was to make. As pesto takes its name from the pestle used to pound it, we used the traditional method and good old-fashioned elbow grease, which made for a delicious, coarse-textured sauce.

Makes 2–4 small jars

50g (1¾oz or ½ cup) Parmesan cheese

200g (7oz) fresh basil leaves, washed and roughly chopped

1 clove of garlic, peeled and finely chopped

½ tsp sea salt

25g (1oz) pine nuts

120ml (4fl oz or ½ cup) extra-virgin olive oil, plus extra for sealing

1. Cut the Parmesan cheese into small pieces as these are easier to grind in the pestle and mortar.

2. Put the basil, garlic and salt into a mortar. Use a pestle to crush the basil and pull the leaves toward you across the mortar to grind the ingredients together. Then add the cheese and the pine nuts and continue to work with the pestle. When they are ground to a texture you like, slowly add the olive oil and work it in to form a paste.

3. Put the pesto into sterilised jars and cover with an extra layer of oil to form a seal. Seal the jars immediately. The pesto will keep for up to three months in the fridge. Stir before using.

Harissa paste

This fiery paste has its origins in North Africa. It is an essential condiment and flavour base in Tunisia, where every family has their homemade version on standby next to the cooking pot. Harissa is traditionally used to accompany lamb or goat.

Makes 1 small jar

50g (1¾oz) dried red chillies

½ tsp coriander seeds

½ tsp cumin seeds

¼ tsp caraway seeds

2 cloves of garlic, peeled and crushed

1 tsp sea salt

2 tsp lemon juice

2–3 tbsp olive oil

1. Put the chillies in a bowl and just cover with boiling water. Leave to soak for a couple of hours. Then remove the chillies from the soaking water (keep this for later) and deseed.

2. Add the coriander, cumin and caraway seeds to a mortar and use the pestle to grind the seeds coarsely.

3. Using either a mini food processor or stick blender, pulse together the chillies, soaking water, garlic, salt and lemon juice.

4. Add the spices from the mortar and give another quick pulse before adding enough olive oil to form a thick, spreadable paste.

5. Spoon into a sterilised jar and seal immediately. The harissa will keep for up to three months in the fridge.

KETCHUPS, MARINADES & DRESSINGS

'And for our home-bred British cheer,
Botargo, catsup and caveer.'

Dr Jonathan Swift, *A Panegyrick on the Dean*, 1730

In *The Art of Cookery made Plain and Easy* (1747), Hannah Glasse dedicates chapter 11 to recipes for captains of ships and begins with a recipe 'to make catchup to keep 20 years'. It is hard to contemplate setting off on a voyage where you might consider that a ketchup that could last you for 20 years would be a good thing, but no doubt its longevity was one of its most appealing qualities in its day, and Mrs Glasse most kindly allows that 'you may carry it to the Indies'. Her recipe uses strong, stale beer (which would essentially have been a vinegar), mushrooms, a pound of anchovies, shallots, ginger, mace, cloves and pepper.

Whereas chutneys originated in India, ketchups come from further northeast. The word 'ketchup' may come from a combination of Chinese and Malay words that were roughly rendered into English as 'catsup', a term used to describe Asian fermented fish sauces. Now, while 'fermented fish sauce' may not sound all that appetising, nor does the rice gruel it was made to accompany and 'pep up', but with their salty taste, concentrated texture and good keeping qualities, these liquid sauces were immensely popular and useful. The original Asian sauces had a high salt content and strong acidity, which enabled them to keep and travel well. This in turn meant that they were much in demand by the Dutch merchants returning from the Orient, who brought them back to Europe at the beginning of the 18th century.

Salted anchovies are frequently found in early ketchup or catsup recipes, the anchovies perhaps replicating the strong salty and fishy flavour of the original ketchups. It may be because of these characteristics that these early ketchups were meant to be used sparingly and were frequently used to form the base of gravies or other sauces.

These days we tend to associate ketchup with tomatoes, but these were a much later addition, introduced mainly after catsup had hit the West. Early ketchups were made from all manner of ingredients, and one of the first recipes for a ketchup in Britain was mushroom ketchup. It is certainly true to say that the products with which the word ketchup is associated have changed much more in their 400-year history than the word itself.

Ketchups and marinades evolved from the same starting process of pickling or fermenting fish, but then developed in different directions. In contrast to modern ketchups, marinades are frequently thinner liquids in which meat or fish is steeped prior to cooking to give extra flavour or to tenderise the meat. A marinade can render a tough and difficult cut of meat soft and tender, and because such cuts of meat tend to have a robust taste of their own, the marinade can complement this by introducing strong and aromatic flavours. Today most marinated foods are grilled or barbecued, so they contain a combination of fat and acid to prevent them from simply burning off before the food is properly cooked.

A good dressing does more than simply dress a 'sallet' – 'salad' to you and me. It can be used as a marinade or to baste meat during cooking. In fact, one of Tracklements' longest-standing customers, a man who has reared and sold meat all his life, swears by using basil vinaigrette to baste a chicken while roasting.

Making ketchups, marinades & dressings

KETCHUPS

Although ketchup has become almost synonymous with tomatoes, in fact it has historically been made from a huge variety of ingredients, such as red peppers, mushrooms, peaches, damsons, walnuts and even oysters and cockles.

A ketchup is a pourable sauce, but unlike a sauce which can contain pieces of fruit or vegetable, a ketchup is smooth, having been passed through a sieve or a mouli. Most chutneys can easily be turned into ketchups by being pressed through a sieve, with perhaps the addition of a little extra vinegar if the resultant purée is then too thick.

Ketchups are made by simply chopping and cooking the featured ingredient and then passing it through a sieve or mouli to extract the purée. This is then simmered gently with vinegar and spices and reduced until the desired consistency is reached, at which point it is poured into sterilised bottles and sealed. The trick comes in balancing the sugar, salt and vinegar with the rest of the ingredients; too heavy a hand will mask the ingredients' flavour and too light a touch will make a ketchup which, although it may taste delicious, won't last long.

Ketchups tend to use spice bags or spiced vinegar to ensure that the flavour of the ketchup straight after cooking is the one it maintains for its life. Using spices in this way also safeguards against grittiness and prevents any powdery residue in the finished ketchup. Free liquid that puddles when the ketchup is poured out indicates that it hasn't been cooked long enough. Tomatoes seem to get hotter than any other ingredient in cooking, so be careful not to splash yourself when boiling these sauces. Using a really big pan should prevent this.

MARINADES

Both the consistency of marinades and their ingredients are determined by the purpose of marinating. If the aim is to tenderise meat or balance the richness of a fatty meat, then the marinade will need a high acid content. If it is to prevent drying out during cooking, then there will be a larger proportion of oil present. If it is simply to impart flavour, then the marinade may contain all manner of ingredients.

As a general rule, marinades rarely contain salt because this draws the moisture out of the meat and will make it tough. The time needed for successful marinating will depend on the size of what is being marinated and also on its texture, as both will influence the speed with which the marinade is absorbed.

DRESSINGS

In order to make the perfect dressing we must force the combination of two naturally reticent allies, sweet oil and sharp vinegar. Once this is achieved, additional flavours are added with mustards, garlic, chilli, spices and herbs.

In order to get the ingredients to blend well, they should all be at room temperature, but a homemade dressing made with good, natural ingredients will always split and will require a good shaking after it has been in the cupboard a while. However, storing it will only improve its flavour. The basic proportions are three parts oil to one part vinegar or lemon juice, beaten or shaken together. The following recipes use a stick blender to achieve emulsification initially which assists the dressing in coating salad leaves, and also means that it will return to being an emulsion more easily when shaken.

The flavour of the oil you use will affect the finished product dramatically, but that doesn't mean you always have to use the most expensive olive oil. There are some dressings that owe their great taste and moreishness to simple sunflower oil. Nowadays there are more varieties and flavours of oil than you can shake a stick at: nut oils, rapeseed oils, olive oil and oils flavoured with truffle oil, chilli or pepper. They all bring their own characteristic flavour to a dressing. Nor does a dressing have to be limited to only one oil; replacing a little sunflower oil with a tablespoon of groundnut oil will subtly change the flavour profile. We use extra-virgin olive oil and sunflower oil because they are lighter, although some extra-virgin olive oils have a very strong 'green' flavour which, while bringing out the very best in some salads, overpowers the delicate flavour of others.

The acid in dressings comes from vinegar or lemon juice, and like the oil, will be a determining factor in the final taste. Again, like the oils, there are a plethora of flavours to choose from: white wine, red wine, sherry, cider, balsamic vinegar, herb, chilli or fruit. We use cider and balsamic vinegar, but there is no necessity to do so. Perhaps it is our heritage as mustard-makers that makes us want to include mustard in our dressings, but they really are a vital element and will give bite and texture and add a delicious and complex element. You don't need much sugar in the dressing, but sugar is an important part of balancing the sharpness of the vinegar.

Real tomato ketchup

Tip

You can use tinned Italian tomatoes instead of fresh, or a combination of both. If using tinned you will need 2½ x 400g tins, including any juice and chopped into quarters.

A Tracklementeer volunteered this cautionary tale. 'On a long, early morning journey I stopped at a roadside diner for a bacon sarnie. When it came, I asked if I could have some tomato ketchup, whereupon I was sternly advised by the waitress that they didn't have tomato ketchup, "only red or brown sauce". After a brief internal struggle, I had to forego the "sauce" and stick to plain old rashers in a bun. Since that day I have always carefully checked that the first ingredient in tomato sauce is "tomato".' This ketchup is a firm favourite in their household.

Makes 2–4 bottles

For the spiced vinegar

200ml (7fl oz or 1 scant cup) cider vinegar

1 tsp cloves

1 tsp black peppercorns

1 tsp (approximately 18) allspice berries

For the ketchup

130ml (4½fl oz or ½ cup) spiced vinegar (above)

1kg (2lb 4oz) fresh plum tomatoes, chopped into quarters

1 large onion, peeled and diced

1 large Bramley apple, peeled, cored and chopped into 2-cm (¾-inch) pieces

15g (½oz or 1 tbsp) sea salt

½ tsp fresh red chilli, deseeded and finely diced

½ tsp freshly ground black pepper

200g (7oz or 1 cup) raw cane sugar

1. First, make the spiced vinegar. Put the vinegar, cloves, peppercorns and allspice berries in a large, heavy-bottomed pan. Bring to the boil and boil for 2 minutes, or until it has reduced by about a third. Remove from the heat and leave to cool while you prepare the rest of the ingredients. Use a slotted spoon to remove the spices from the vinegar and discard. Measure out 130ml (4½fl oz or ½ cup) of the spiced vinegar and return to the pan.

2. Add the tomatoes, onion, apple and salt to the vinegar. Bring the mixture to the boil, stirring occasionally. After 10 minutes or so the tomatoes should have released their juices and the apple should be soft enough to squash against the side of the pan using the back of the spoon. Stir in the chilli and black pepper.

3. Transfer to a blender (or a high-sided bowl or jug if using a stick blender) and whizz the mixture until it is smooth. Press it through a sieve to extract the tomato pips, skins and any pieces of onion, leaving a really smooth purée. It is worth scraping a spatula across the underside of the sieve to make sure that none of the delicious mixture is missed.

4. Put the sieved mixture back in the cleaned pan and add the sugar, stirring continuously over a medium heat until all the sugar has dissolved. Boil for 20–30 minutes, or until you like the look of the consistency. You will need to stir it more towards the end of the cooking time to make sure it doesn't catch on the bottom of the pan. The right consistency has been reached when your ketchup is thick enough so that it doesn't just run off the back of the spoon and there is no puddling on the surface.

5. Use a funnel to pour into sterilised bottles and seal immediately.

Homemade tomato purée

Many of the following recipes use a tomato purée as their base and it is such a useful building block for all sorts of foods such as pasta sauces and pizza toppings. Homemade tomato purée is not as thick and paste-like as store-bought, which is usually double concentrate. If you find you haven't enough homemade purée for a recipe requiring it, you can always supplement it by boiling down tinned tomatoes or using shop-bought purée.

Makes 2–4 bottles of rich purée

2kg (4lb 8oz) or approximately 20 ripe plum tomatoes

1. Cut the tomatoes into quarters and place in a large, heavy-bottomed preserving pan.

2. Cook over a medium–high heat for 30–40 minutes, or until the tomatoes are really mushy, stirring occasionally. They will essentially boil in their own juice.

3. Pour the tomato mush into a sieve over a bowl and gently rub the mixture through the sieve with the back of a wooden spoon or a spatula. It takes some time to press all the juice through, and it helps if occasionally you scrape the underside of the sieve with a spatula to make sure you capture all the purée.

4. Rinse the preserving pan and return the tomato purée to it. Bring to the boil and continue to boil for 30–40 minutes, or until it has thickened and reduced by half. You will need to stir it more frequently towards the end to stop it from sticking to the bottom of the pan.

5. Pour into sterilised bottles and seal immediately.

Barbecue sauce

A food writer and friend of Tracklements wrote about this ketchup,
'If you've never tasted a premium ketchup, you really must. It is like
driving an Aston Martin after spending your life chugging around in a
Fiat Panda.' We would love to agree, but no one has yet let us try out an
Aston Martin so we will have to take her word for it!

This unctuous concoction is richly tomato-ey, with warming, spicy
overtones and just cries out to be dolloped onto chunky chips or a tasty
homemade burger.

Makes 2–4 bottles

3–4 dried bird's-eye chillies or ¼
tsp dried crushed chillies

½ tsp (approximately 9) allspice
berries

½ tsp black peppercorns

1 medium onion, peeled and
roughly chopped

2 cloves of garlic, peeled and
roughly chopped

450ml (16fl oz or 2 cups)
cider vinegar

2 tsp sea salt

2 tsp lemon juice

340g (12oz or scant 1¾ cups)
raw cane sugar

600g (1lb 5oz) tomato purée
(see page 142)

1. Grind the chillies and spices together, using either a pestle and mortar or
a mini food processor to ensure that all their essential oils are kept.

2. Add the onion and garlic to a food processor and whizz together to make
a paste. Put the paste into a large, heavy-bottomed preserving pan, add the
vinegar and bring to the boil. Lower the heat and allow to simmer for 5
minutes to give the onion time to cook.

3. Add the chilli and ground spice mixture, salt and lemon juice and give
everything a really good stir. Add the sugar and stir well until it is has
completely dissolved.

4. Add the tomato purée, stirring well to mix. Bring to the boil for 20–30
minutes, or until a thick consistency is reached. The ketchup will do its best
to resemble a volcano and bubble and spit when boiling, so be careful not to
get spattered.

5. Pour into sterilised bottles and seal immediately.

Brown sauce

This fruity brown sauce started life as 'Cab-shelter Sauce' and was favoured by London's Hansom cab drivers to have with their meat, chops or eggs. Rich, dark brown and deliciously tangy, its popularity hasn't faltered to this day.

Makes 2–4 bottles

300ml (10fl oz or 1¼ cups) cider vinegar

180ml (6fl oz or generous ¾ cup) soy sauce

1 small onion, peeled and chopped

8 cloves of garlic, peeled

20g (¾oz or approximately 2 tbsp) dried seedless dates, chopped

1 large fresh red chilli, deseeded and diced

½ fresh green chilli, deseeded and diced

15g (½oz) or approximately 1 tbsp tamarind paste

1 tsp sea salt

330g (11½oz or 1⅔ cups) raw cane sugar

600g (1lb 5oz) tomato purée (see page 142)

10ml (2 tsp) lemon juice

1. Gently heat the vinegar and soy sauce in a large, heavy-bottomed saucepan over a medium heat. Put the onion, garlic and dates into a food processor and whizz to form a paste, then add this to the pan and stir. Bring to the boil, lower the heat and simmer for 5 minutes.

2. Add the chillies, tamarind paste and salt to the pan and mix well. Bring to the boil and slowly add the sugar, stirring well to make sure it has completely dissolved.

3. Add the tomato purée and lemon juice, and bring back to the boil for 20–30 minutes, or until the desired consistency is reached. Pour into sterilised bottles and seal immediately.

Sweet mustard ketchup

...or 'yellow devil sauce', as we call it, goes with just about everything and is the perfect mopper-up of leftovers. We made it because we wanted a piquant sauce in which to marinate meat, but then discovered how very good it is simply poured over sausages, potato salad or pieces of cold chicken.

Makes 2–5 bottles

500g (1lb 2oz) strong English mustard

250g (9oz) wholegrain mustard

225ml (8fl oz or 1 cup) cider vinegar

400g (14oz or 2 cups) raw cane sugar

15g (½oz or 1 tbsp) sea salt

25g (4 tbsp) ground turmeric

150ml (5fl oz or ⅔ cup) sunflower oil

1. Put the mustards in a blender and pulse. Add the vinegar, sugar, salt and turmeric and pulse for a couple more seconds.

2. With the blender running on the slowest setting, gradually add the oil until it emulsifies.

3. Pour the ketchup into sterilised bottles and seal immediately. Shake well before serving.

Mushroom ketchup

Although we don't produce a mushroom ketchup, our curiosity was piqued by the knowledge that this was the first ketchup made in the UK. Certainly when we started rifling through our cookbook library we found that the older the cookbook, the more likely it was to contain a mushroom ketchup recipe. Modern books tend to ignore it, or have changed it dramatically into a thick sauce, whereas this authentic recipe makes a thin, almost black, liquid sauce that's great for adding to stews and gravy. You need to prepare the mushrooms and spice vinegar the day before you make the actual ketchup.

Large field mushrooms are best, as they have a better flavour than cultivated button mushrooms. They must be perfectly dry; don't be tempted to wash a mushroom – if there's any dirt on them, just rub it off with kitchen towel.

Makes 1–2 bottles

1.35kg (3lb) large field mushrooms, skins and stalks included, diced quite finely

40g (1½oz or 2 heaped tbsp) sea salt

300ml (10fl oz or 1¼ cups) spiced vinegar

1 medium onion, peeled and diced

For the spiced vinegar

300ml (10fl oz or 1¼ cups) malt vinegar

1 tsp black peppercorns

1 tsp (approximately 18) allspice berries

1 tsp cloves

1 tsp ground ginger

6 dried bird's-eye chillies

1. Layer the diced mushrooms in a large bowl, sprinkling salt between each layer. Cover and leave for 24 hours.

2. Make the spiced vinegar by combining the vinegar, spices and chillies in a small saucepan and bring just to the boil. Remove the pan from the heat and set aside overnight, allowing the spices to infuse.

3. The next day, remove the spices from the vinegar with a slotted spoon and discard. Put the spiced vinegar, onion, mushrooms and their juices into a large pan and bring to the boil, then cover, lower the heat and simmer gently for 2 hours. Remove from the heat and allow to cool for 10 minutes.

4. Strain through a doubled muslin placed over a sieve on top of a measuring jug or bowl. Give the muslin a squeeze to make sure all the juice is extracted.

5. Return the juice to the pan and bring back to the boil. When it is hot pour into sterilised bottles and seal immediately.

Pontack catsup

During their fleeting September season, ripe, purple elderberries hang down from wild hedgerows, begging to be picked and transformed into this powerful, fruity concoction that perfectly suits game, pork or offal. The somewhat unusual name is said to come from the sauce's inventor, François-Auguste de Pontac, who opened the first 'fashionable, genteel eating house' in London immediately after the Great Fire of 1666. Reputed and celebrated as a superb French cook, de Pontac left a lasting legacy in the form of this sauce, which takes the older British spelling (adding a 'K') and gives a welcome belt of flavour to gravies and casseroles.

Early recipes demanded that this sauce should be kept for seven years before opening. It is certainly true that it improves with age, so making a batch each year will ensure that you always have some to hand.

Tip
Run a fork down the elderberry stalk to remove the berries.

Makes 1 bottle

500g (1lb 2oz) elderberries

500ml (18fl oz or 2¼ cups) cider vinegar

200g (7oz) shallots, peeled and finely diced

15g (½oz) fresh ginger root, peeled and finely chopped

6 cloves

1 blade (½ tsp) mace

½ tsp black peppercorns

1. Preheat the oven to 100°C/200°F/gas mark ¼.

2. Put the berries and vinegar in an ovenproof dish with a tight-fitting lid. Bake in the oven overnight (approximately 8 hours).

3. Strain the juice through muslin laid over a sieve into a heavy-bottomed pan. Add the finely diced shallots, ginger and spices and bring to a vigorous boil. Boil for 10–15 minutes.

4. Strain the juice into sterilised bottles and seal immediately. Shake well before serving.

Basil vinaigrette

The perfect dressing for a fresh tomato salad – 'nuff said!

Makes 1–2 bottles

150ml (5fl oz or ⅔ cup)
cider vinegar

1 clove of garlic, peeled
and crushed

a handful of fresh basil leaves,
washed and roughly chopped

1tsp green peppercorns

2 tsp brown mustard seeds

375ml (13fl oz or 1⅔ cups)
olive oil

2 tsp raw cane sugar

1 tsp sea salt

25g (1oz or 1½ tbsp)
Dijon mustard

1. Put half the vinegar with the garlic, basil and green peppercorns in a blender and whizz for a couple of seconds until the peppercorns are smashed up and the basil is in flecks. Add the remaining vinegar.

2. Pound the mustard seeds with a pestle and mortar just enough to open them, then add them along with half the oil and all the sugar to the blender and pulse again.

3. Add the salt, Dijon mustard and the remaining oil to the blender and give a final whizz to make sure everything is well mixed.

4. Pour the vinaigrette into sterilised bottles immediately and seal. Shake well before serving.

Herb vinaigrette

This is a great vinaigrette if you need to add interest to an otherwise plain salad. It's also really useful for basting meat while cooking.

Makes 1–2 bottles

130ml (4½fl oz or generous ½ cup) cider vinegar

a handful of fresh dill leaves, washed

a handful of fresh parsley leaves, washed

a handful of fresh tarragon leaves, washed

2 tsp raw cane sugar

1 tsp wholegrain mustard

1 tsp Dijon mustard

1 tsp sea salt

Pinch of freshly ground black pepper

375ml (13fl oz or 1⅔ cups) olive oil

1. Put half the vinegar in a blender with the herbs and whizz until they're in small flecks. Add the rest of the vinegar, the sugar, mustards, salt and pepper and give another whizz to mix everything together.

2. With the blender running on the slowest setting, gradually add the oil until it emulsifies.

3. Pour the vinaigrette into sterilised bottles immediately and seal. Shake well before serving.

Salad dressing

This is a really good example of an original, authentic French dressing, the perfect accompaniment to a simple green salad. What gives it its tangy flavour is the tarragon, a favourite in French cuisine but which can have its detractors, too. Many people think they don't like tarragon, but when used in small quantities, as here, most people cannot identify it and just get on with enjoying the dressing. The proportions of oil to vinegar are vital and the use of both olive and sunflower oils gives this dressing a light taste.

Makes 1–2 bottles

½ tsp fresh tarragon leaves

130ml (4½fl oz or generous ½ cup) cider vinegar

1 large clove of garlic, peeled and crushed

3 heaped tbsp Dijon mustard

2 tsp raw cane sugar

1 tsp sea salt

Pinch of freshly ground black pepper

180ml (6fl oz or generous ¾ cup) olive oil

200ml (7fl oz or scant 1 cup) sunflower oil

1. Chop the tarragon leaves really finely; don't give up until they are just minuscule flecks, then add them to the vinegar. Alternatively, whizz them with the vinegar using a stick blender.

2. Add the garlic, mustard, sugar, salt and black pepper and give the vinaigrette another quick whizz.

3. With the blender running on the slowest setting, gradually add the oils until they emulsify, giving you a beautifully smooth, creamy dressing. If decanting your dressing into more than one container, do it immediately to prevent it from separating differently between the bottles. Seal.

4. Shake well before serving.

Tomato & chilli dressing

This is a great dressing to give a bit of Mediterranean oomph to mozzarella salads or to use as a marinade. The tomatoes give it sweetness and the chilli gives it some heat.

Makes 1–2 bottles

200ml (7fl oz or scant 1 cup) cider vinegar

25g (1oz or 2 tbsp) raw cane sugar

½ fresh red chilli, deseeded and very finely chopped

1 clove of garlic, peeled and crushed

1 tsp fresh lemon juice

Pinch of freshly ground black pepper

1 tsp sea salt

3 tbsp tomato purée concentrate

1 tsp Dijon mustard

Pinch of smoked paprika

250ml (9fl oz or 1 cup + 2 tbsp) sunflower oil

1. Put all the ingredients except the oil in a suitable container and either whizz with a stick blender, stir or put a lid on and shake until mixed together.

2. With the blender running on the slowest setting, gradually add the oil until it emulsifies and you have a smooth dressing.

3. Pour into sterilised bottles immediately and seal.

4. Shake well before serving.

Balsamic vinaigrette

We met the Giacobazzi family at a food fair in Italy and immediately felt like we'd found like-minded souls who work hard to make sure their aged balsamic vinegar tastes excellent. This vinaigrette perfectly marries the tang of balsamic vinegar with olive oil to make a dressing that any tricolore salad would be proud of.

Makes 1–2 bottles

130ml (4½fl oz or generous ½ cup) balsamic vinegar

1 tsp raw cane sugar

1 tsp sea salt

1 clove of garlic, peeled and crushed

2 tsp Dijon mustard

Pinch of freshly ground black pepper

375ml (13fl oz or 1⅔ cups) olive oil

1. Put the vinegar in a blender and add the sugar, salt, garlic, mustard and pepper. Give a good 10-second whizz. Then, with the blender running on the slowest setting, gradually add the oil until it emulsifies.

2. Pour the vinaigrette into sterilised bottles immediately and seal. Shake well before serving.

Honey mustard vinaigrette

Mustard is our heartland at Tracklements and try as we might we just want to include it in everything, so here is a dressing which does just that. We think it's the perfect way to dress an avocado.

Makes 1–2 bottles

160ml (5½fl oz or generous ⅔ cup) cider vinegar

15g (½oz or 1 tbsp) raw cane sugar

45g (1½oz or 3 tbsp) wholegrain mustard

1 heaped tsp sea salt

3 tbsp runny honey

375ml (13fl oz or 1⅔ cups) olive oil

1. Put the vinegar in a blender. Add the sugar, mustard and salt and give it a good 10-second whizz. Add the honey and give the mixture another blast.

2. With the blender running on the slowest setting, gradually add the oil until it emulsifies.

3. Pour the vinaigrette into sterilised bottles immediately and seal. Shake well before serving.

SAVOURY JELLIES, CHEESES & FRUIT BUTTERS

'Fruit jellies are some of the most useful preserves. Most
people consider that roast game birds or venison served without
redcurrant, crab apple or rowan jelly would lack a very important
accompaniment.'
Marguerite Patten, *The Basic Basics Handbook: Jams, Preserves
and Chutneys*, 1995

Quite apart from wanting to store the July harvest for the January larder, savoury
jellies typify the 'Waste not, want not' attitudes of past generations. Allowing
vitamin-rich and potentially tasty fruits to rot on the ground was unthinkable, and
it behove conscientious cooks to gather surplus yields and turn their hands to the
culinary alchemy of transforming the unpalatable into the indispensable.

Savoury jellies most frequently feature fruits that either produce extravagantly
during the season or would otherwise have been inedible; indeed, this was how bitter,
unappetising Seville oranges became transformed into the much-loved marmalades
we enjoy today. Unripe, windfall apples or crab apples, bullaces, medlars and sloes,
while all indigestible when first picked, will give up their flavours when boiled
in water and create the most magnificent jellies when mixed with sugar.

Jellies have played an important role throughout history. During the Industrial Revolution, when there was an exodus of the population from countryside to town, it was virtually impossible to transport enough fresh produce into towns and cities, so preserves remained important. During the two world wars when rationing ruled the kitchens, jam- and jelly-makers were allowed larger rations of sugar to keep the flow of jelly-making going.

Commercial jams began to appear during the 19th century, although most jellies were still made only by domestic cooks. When Tracklements introduced the first of range of jellies – Apple & Mint, Apple & Sage and Apple & Thyme – in the early 1970s, they were the first commercial examples of their kind.

However, not content with creating just one delicious condiment from harvested fruit, households frequently made use of the leftover fruit pulp to make a set fruit preserve called a 'cheese'; consequently, jellies and cheeses have been intimately linked together in the history of fruit preservation. Between them they ensure that nothing of the fruit is wasted. The last word in thrift and recycling, these solid-set bursts of fruit used not only the remainders of fruit from jelly-making but it is also suggested that the description 'cheese' comes from an historical habit of reusing old cheese moulds to make them in. Fruit butters have their origins in Europe, and the Dutch today have similar products – in fact, it was the colonising Dutch who made butters so popular in the US, where they are used much more as a sweet spread. While cheeses are set preserves, fruit butters have a thick, but soft, spreadable consistency. Smoother and thicker than a jam, they contain less sugar than other savoury preserves or cheeses and are cooked for less time which results in a shorter shelf life.

Making savoury jellies, cheeses & fruit butters

Time and timing are vital ingredients in making a good jelly. There are two main stages: neither can be hurried but both need to happen in a timely fashion. The aim is to make a jelly that is bright both in taste and colour – clear, with a good, firm set and packing a fruity wallop to enrich the flavour of the meat with which it is most often served.

The best jellies are made with firm fruit; as a rule, slightly under-ripe is better than over-ripe. Give the fruit a once-over to check for blemishes and bugs – the odd scratch doesn't matter, but bad bruises are best avoided. The easiest jellies to make use fruit containing high levels of natural pectin – this is what makes the jelly set. These are fruits such as cooking apples, redcurrants or gooseberries, which is why they are most often used to make herb jellies and to assist jellies containing ingredients that have no pectin of their own. Hard fruit needs to be chopped into smaller pieces prior to boiling, but soft fruits can be put in whole, as they will give up their juice more easily.

Fruit stores its natural pectin in its skin, pith, seeds and stalks. However, pectin starts to break down gently from the moment the fruit is harvested, which is why it's always better to use freshly picked fruit for jelly-making. Freezing fruit breaks down pectin, which makes getting a set more difficult, although not impossible. Some purists will argue that you should remove all the stalks beforehand because they may give a bitter taste, but we don't find they make a significant difference. Another ingredient added to most jellies is lemon juice. This not only adds flavour but also helps the release of pectin.

At Tracklements, we always use granulated raw cane sugar, which experience has taught us gives the best, most vibrant colour. The key to making a successful jelly that will set and keep well is to use an equal amount of sugar to fruit juice. So, the first stage of jelly-making is to make the fruit juice. As a rule of thumb, you will need 1 litre (1¾ pints or 4 cups) of water to 1 kilo (2lb 4oz) of fruit.

When it comes to the boiling, it's important not to over-boil at any stage. In the first stage the fruit should be simmered with water just until it has released its juice and turned mushy. During the second, preserving stage – boiling the juice with sugar – a vigorous, rolling boil is needed so that the sugar doesn't caramelise, which would create a dark jelly and possibly

How to tell if your jelly will set

Drop a little of the hot jelly mixture onto a chilled saucer, count to 10, then push the jelly with your fingertip. If the jelly crinkles, then setting point has been reached. If setting point hasn't been reached, return the pan to the heat and continue boiling, testing every minute or two until the jelly crinkles on the saucer.

a burnt taste. At the end we use a small sieve or slotted spoon to remove the scum from the top of the mixture. Historically this scum was a result of impurities in the sugar, but now it's really a result of bubbly sugar and fruit, and it is more unsightly than objectionable.

All the jelly recipes will make 4–6 jars from 1 litre (1¾ pints or 4 cups) of juice. While sterilising the jars is good practice, we don't think it's entirely necessary with jellies, as you're generally putting in something that is so hot it will do the sterilising as it goes in. A 500ml (18fl oz or 2¼ cup) plastic jug with a narrow spout or a funnel makes filling the jars quickly and without mess, which in turn means you can get the lid on before it gets too hot to handle; it also helps to stop bubbles from forming in the finished jar. If air bubbles do form, gently tap the jars just after filling to get rid of them. If you're making a jelly that has pieces of herb or spices suspended in it, you will need to let it cool for 2–5 minutes before pouring it into the jars; otherwise all the herbs and spices will float to the surface. Once filled, put the lids on. Separate the jars and allow them to cool naturally to give a lovely, firm texture. Jellies made in this way will have at least a year's shelf life.

If your jelly hasn't set, don't despair, but don't try to reboil it at this point. Instead – and in true British fashion – make the best of it. Put it in the fridge and enjoy eating it poured over ice cream, or dilute it with fizzy water and use it as a cordial. If it's not that sort of jelly, then try adding it to stews or gravy for added oomph.

CHEESES AND FRUIT BUTTERS

Fruit cheeses have a delightful, grainy texture and intense flavour and are truly fantastic on the cheeseboard. Although originally made with leftovers they (somewhat obviously) taste stronger and better if made using fresh fruit dedicated to the purpose. Fruit butters are also made with fruit but have the consistency of soft butter, hence their name.

Usually made with high-pectin fruit such as quince, damson or gooseberry, fruit cheese is simple to make and involves boiling sieved fruit pulp together with sugar in order to create a concentrated fruit preserve that brings a taste of summer to every cheeseboard.

Fruit butters use orchard fruits such as pear, apple, apricot and peach, either individually or a mixture, and are a great way of using fruit without the chore of peeling and coring. We always use a little spice, such as cinnamon, cloves or allspice, in our fruit butters to make a savoury accompaniment. Use either a spice bag (in which case double the quantities), or grind using a pestle and mortar. Chilli can be used for the adventurous and a favourite of ours is apple and chilli butter!

Redcurrant jelly

There are lots of reasons to wax lyrical about redcurrants: both the plants and the fruit. The plants are pretty and easy to grow, thriving as they do in difficult areas in the garden and being impervious to our cooler climate. Their fruit is sharp, sweet and packed with vitamin C and other goodly things, as well as pectin. But it has a regrettably short season (July), which makes redcurrants the perfect fruit for preserving. This jelly is known as 'lamb jam' at Tracklements, although is used in a multitude of other ways: from a spoonful in gravies to accompanying roast chicken or, when occasion demands, just spread on a crumpet!

Makes 4–6 jars per 1 litre (1¼ pints or 4 cups) of juice

For the juice

1kg (2lb 4oz) redcurrants

500ml (18fl oz or 2¼ cups) water

For the jelly – for each 1 litre (1¼ pints or 4 cups) of juice use

1kg (2lb 4oz or 5 cups) raw cane sugar

25ml (1fl oz or 1 tbsp + 2 tsp) lemon juice

1. Rinse the redcurrants but don't bother taking them off the stalks; just put them in a large pan with the water and bring to the boil. Lower the heat and simmer for 30 minutes until the fruit is soft and mushy. Remove from the heat and pour the juice into a jelly bag or doubled muslin suspended over a measuring jug or bowl. Leave between 3 hours and overnight (but no longer than 24 hours) to let the juice strain through at its own gentle pace. Don't be tempted to squeeze the juice through; this will make your jelly cloudy.

2. The next step is to measure the redcurrant juice; this recipe should give you about 1 litre (1¼ pints or 4 cups). Measure out the sugar and lemon juice. At this point put your saucer in the fridge to test for setting point later on.

3. Put the redcurrant juice and sugar into a large, heavy-bottomed preserving pan and heat gently, stirring constantly until all the sugar has dissolved, then bring to a rolling boil. Add the lemon juice and bring back to a vigorous, rolling boil. Boil until the mixture reaches setting point – this should be after about 20 minutes. To test for setting point, remove the pan from the heat, drop a little of the jelly mixture onto the cold saucer, count to 10 and push it with your fingertip. If the jelly wrinkles then setting point has been reached. If setting point hasn't been reached, return the pan to the heat and continue boiling, testing every minute or two until the jelly crinkles on the saucer.

4. Remove from the heat, skim off any scum on the surface using a small sieve or slotted spoon and spoon into sterilised jars. Put the lids on immediately. Separate the jars and leave to cool.

Medlar jelly

While researching for a film, our friend Simon Channing Williams stayed in a pub just down the road from Tracklements. In the beer garden was a fruit tree laden with fruit that he had never seen before. With the landlord's permission he picked a bucketful and set off to research what they were and what culinary use they could be put to. The result is medlar jelly, a particularly aromatic jelly that's perfect with game.

In medieval times, medlars were called 'pigs' or 'dogs' bottoms', which, while very rude, is also accurate when you look at them. Medlars are harvested in October, after the first frost, and the best medlar jelly is made from a combination of medlars that have gone slightly soft and squishy and some that are still hard.

Tip
If your medlars are rock-hard, lay them out on newspaper in a cool room and leave to ripen for a week or two.

Makes 4–6 jars per 1 litre (1¼ pints or 4 cups) of juice

For the juice
1kg (2lb 4oz) medlars, leaves removed and cut into quarters

1 litre (1¾ pints or 4 cups) water

1 lemon, cut into quarters

For the jelly – for each 1 litre (1¼ pints or 4 cups) of juice use
1kg (2lb 4oz or 5 cups) raw cane sugar

To test for setting point
Drop a little of the jelly mixture onto a cold saucer, count to 10 and push it with your fingertip. If the jelly wrinkles then setting point has been reached.

1. Put the medlars into a large, heavy-bottomed preserving pan and pour the water over the top. Add the lemon quarters to the pan. Bring to the boil, then cover, lower the heat and reduce to a simmer, stirring occasionally. Simmer gently for 40 minutes, or until the fruit has turned to a pulp.

2. Pour the fruit mash into a jelly bag or doubled muslin suspended over a measuring jug or bowl. Leave between 3 hours and overnight (but no longer than 24 hours) to let the juice strain through at its own gentle pace. Don't squeeze the juice through if you want a beautifully clear jelly. When the juice has filtered through your kitchen will smell wonderfully fragrant and sweet.

3. The next step is to measure the medlar juice and sugar. You will need an equal amount of sugar to liquid, so if you've got 700ml (24fl oz or generous 3 cups) of liquid you will need 700g (1lb 9oz or generous 3 cups) of sugar. At this point put your saucer in the fridge to test the setting point later on.

4. Put the juice and sugar into a large, heavy-bottomed preserving pan and heat gently, stirring constantly until the sugar has dissolved, then bring to a rolling boil. Boil until the mixture reaches setting point – this should take about 20 minutes – then remove from the heat. If setting point hasn't been reached, return the pan to the heat and continue boiling, testing every minute or two until the jelly wrinkles on the saucer.

5. Remove from the heat, skim off any scum on the surface and pour into sterilised jars. Seal immediately. Separate the jars and leave to cool.

Gooseberry & elderflower jelly

Tip

Use slightly under-ripe
gooseberries if possible
for this recipe.

There are few pairings that go together as well as tart, green
gooseberries and sweet, fragrant elderflowers, which appear together
for a brief time in early summer. The Tracklements HQ is positioned on
the Fosse Way, an ancient Roman road that links Exeter to Lincoln and
a beautiful place for a spring stroll. Our stretch of Wiltshire Fosse is
lined with elder trees that burst into flower every May.

*Makes 4–6 jars per 1 litre
(1¼ pints or 4 cups) of juice*

For the juice

1kg (2lb 4oz) whole
gooseberries, washed

Water to cover: approximately
750ml (26fl oz 3⅓ cups)

15 elderflower heads
(approximately 100g/3½oz)

*For the jelly – for each
1 litre (1¼ pints or 4 cups)
of juice use*

1kg (2lb 4oz or 5 cups) raw
cane sugar

25ml (1fl oz or 1 tbsp + 2 tsp)
lemon juice

1. Put the gooseberries into a large pan with just enough water to cover.
Bring to the boil, stirring occasionally, lower the heat and simmer for
30 minutes, or until the fruit is soft and pulpy. Remove from the heat and
add the elderflower heads. Stir gently and leave for about 1 hour to allow
the elderflowers to infuse the juice.

2. Pour the fruit pulp into a jelly bag or doubled muslin and place in a sieve
suspended over a measuring jug or bowl. Leave to strain for between
3 hours and overnight. Do not leave for more than 24 hours, though, or you
will struggle to get a set.

3. Then measure the juice and weigh out an equal amount of sugar; so
for 900ml (32fl oz or 4 cups) juice, add 900g (2lb or 4½ cups) of sugar and
22.5ml (1 tablespoon) of lemon juice. Put your saucer in the fridge ready
for testing the setting point later on.

4. Put the juice and sugar into a large, heavy-bottomed preserving pan and
heat gently, stirring constantly, until all the sugar has dissolved. Bring to
a rolling boil. Add the lemon juice. Boil until the mixture reaches setting
point – this should take about 10 minutes – test for set (see left), then
remove from the heat and skim off any scum on the surface. If setting
point hasn't been reached, return the pan to the heat and continue boiling,
testing every minute or two until the jelly wrinkles on the saucer.

5. Remove from the heat, skim off any scum on the surface and pour
into sterilised jars. Put the lids on immediately. Separate the jars and
leave to cool.

Damson jelly

The forager's dream, damsons are our native versions of plums and grow freely in hedgerows, as well as being prized for their blossom in gardens. Their deep, purply-blue skins look dusty and tempt you to rub your thumb over them. They have large stones and wild ones render some great gurning if eaten raw, although this never seems to bother the wasps that will feast on them if you leave them on the tree to ripen. But that's OK because for jelly-making slightly under-ripe damsons are best.

Damsons are so generous with their flavour that not only do they make a delicious jelly, but the leftover fruit pulp makes a fantastically fruity cheese.

Makes 4–6 jars per 1 litre (1¼ pints or 4 cups) of juice

For the juice

1kg (2lb 4oz) firm damsons

Enough water to cover: approximately 750ml– 1 litre (1½–1¾ pints or 3⅓–4 cups)

For the jelly – for each 1 litre (1¼ pints or 4 cups) of juice use

1kg (2lb 4oz or 5 cups) raw cane sugar

25ml (1fl oz or 1 tbsp + 2 tsp) lemon juice

1. Check the damsons for bugs and bruising, then put them in a large, heavy-bottomed preserving pan and pour the water over the top just to cover the fruit. Bring to the boil, cover, lower the heat and simmer for 30 minutes, or until the fruit is mushy. Pour the contents of the pan into a jelly bag or doubled muslin suspended over a measuring jug or bowl. Leave for between 3 hours and overnight (but no longer than 24 hours) for the juice to strain through gently at its own pace.

2. If you wish, you can now set aside the fruit pulp for cheese-making (see page 178). Measure the juice. You will need an equal amount of sugar to liquid, so if you have 1 litre (1¾ pints or 4 cups) of juice you will need 1kg (2lb 4oz or 5 cups) of sugar and 25ml (1fl oz or 1 tablespoon + 2 teaspoons) of lemon juice. Put a saucer in the fridge for testing the setting point.

3. Put the juice and sugar into a large, heavy-bottomed preserving pan and heat gently, stirring regularly to dissolve the sugar. Bring to a rolling boil. Add the lemon juice and bring back to the boil, stirring constantly. Keep it at a rolling boil until setting point is reached – this should take about 10 minutes. To test for setting point, drop a little of the jelly mixture onto the cold saucer, count to 10 and push it with your fingertip to see if it wrinkles. If setting point hasn't been reached, return the pan to the heat and continue boiling, testing every minute or two until the jelly crinkles on the saucer.

4. Once setting point is reached, remove from the heat, skim any scum from the surface and pour into sterilised jars. Put the lids on immediately. Separate the jars and leave to cool.

Crab apple jelly

Crab apples are usually found growing wild in abundance along paths and on the edge of old woodlands, away from modern farms. The small, inedible apples weigh down the boughs of the hoary old trees. Every September we choose a fine day and head out with pupils from our local school to collect crates and crates of this under-rated fruit from around our Cotswold village. We then take our haul of scabby, misshapen, incredibly tart fruit to the school and show the students how to cook them up into a delicious, sweet, mellow jelly.

Makes 4–6 jars per 1 litre
(1¼ pints or 4 cups) of juice
For the juice
1kg (2lb 4oz) crab apples

1 litre (1¾ pints or 4 cups) water

For the jelly – for each
1 litre (1¼ pints or 4 cups)
of juice use
1kg (2lb 4oz or 5 cups) raw
cane sugar
25ml (1fl oz or 1 tbsp + 2 tsp)
lemon juice

1. Check the crab apples to ensure they're bug- and bruise-free. Chop roughly into halves (or quarters if they're big crab apples). Put in a large pan and cover with the water. Bring to the boil, cover, lower the heat and simmer for 20 minutes, or until the apples have turned to mush. Remove from the heat and pour the mash through a jelly bag or doubled muslin suspended over a measuring jug or bowl. Leave for a minimum of 3 hours, or overnight (but no longer than 24 hours) until all the juice has strained through under its own weight. Don't be tempted to squeeze the muslin or push the mash through if you want a beautifully clear jelly.

2. Measure the juice. You should have about 1 litre (1¾ pints or 4 cups) of beautifully pale-pink juice scenting your kitchen. Measure out an equal weight of sugar to juice and put them both into a large, heavy-bottomed preserving pan. Put a saucer in the fridge for the setting-point test. Heat the juice gently, stirring constantly until all the sugar has dissolved, then bring to a rolling boil. Add the lemon juice and bring back to a rolling boil, stirring occasionally.

3. Boil the mixture until setting point is reached, usually about 20 minutes. To test for setting point, drop a little of the jelly mixture onto the cold saucer, count to 10 and push it with your fingertip to see if it wrinkles. If setting point hasn't been reached, return the pan to the heat and continue boiling, testing every minute or two until the jelly wrinkles on the saucer.

4. Once setting point is reached, remove from the heat, skim any scum from the surface with a sieve or slotted spoon and pour into sterilised jars. Put the lids on immediately. Separate the jars and leave to cool.

Chilli & lemongrass jelly

Exotic, aromatic, warming and flavoursome, this vibrant jelly reflects our British enthusiasm for adopting and adapting food from around the world. It is a delicious accompaniment to salmon, haddock fishcakes or added to a stir-fry. You're going to love it.

Makes 4–6 jars per 1 litre (1¼ pints or 4 cups) of juice

For the juice

2 lemongrass stalks, bashed and chopped into 2.5-cm (1-inch) pieces

1kg (2lb 4oz) unwaxed lemons (about 10–11, depending on size), cut into quarters

1.5 litres (about 3 pints or 6⅓ cups) water

For the jelly – for each 1 litre (1¼ pints or 4 cups) of juice use

1kg (2lb 4oz or 5 cups) raw cane sugar

1 fresh red chilli, deseeded and very finely chopped

1 fresh green chilli, deseeded and very finely chopped

10g (¼oz) fresh ginger root, peeled and diced

2 cloves of garlic, peeled and diced

10g (¼oz) fresh coriander leaves, washed and finely chopped

1. Put the lemongrass and lemons in a large pan and cover with the water. Bring to the boil, cover and simmer for 1 hour, or until the lemons are pulpy. Remove from the heat and pour through a jelly bag or doubled muslin suspended over a measuring jug or bowl. Leave for between 3 hours and overnight (but no longer than 24 hours). Remember not to squeeze the muslin or your jelly will end up cloudy.

2. When all the juice has drained out, measure it and weigh out an equal amount of sugar. The juice will appear milky and should have a strong, clean, citrus aroma. Put a saucer in the fridge for the setting test later on.

3. Put the sugar and juice into a large, heavy-bottomed preserving pan and heat gently, stirring constantly until all the sugar has dissolved, then bring to a rolling boil. Boil until the liquid reaches setting point – between 10 and 20 minutes. You can tell when to start testing for a set when the liquid turns from opaque to clear and doesn't run off the edge of your wooden spoon quite as quickly when lifted out of the mix.

4. To test the set, drop a little of the jelly onto the cold saucer, count to 10 and push it with your fingertip. If the jelly wrinkles, then setting point has been reached. Once setting point has been reached, remove from the heat and leave for a minute before skimming off any scum on the surface with a small sieve or slotted spoon.

5. Add the chopped or diced chillies, ginger, garlic and coriander leaves and give a gentle but thorough stir to mix through. Stir very gently every 2 minutes, while the jelly starts to cool to ensure the pieces are evenly distributed throughout and don't all rise to the surface.

6. When the jelly has cooled enough so that it's still liquid but the pieces have stopped rising (about 5–10 minutes), pour into sterilised jars and put on the lids immediately. Separate the jars and leave to cool.

Lemon & thyme jelly

One of our customers has an area called 'The Thyme Walk' in the garden and asked if we could make a jelly featuring this aromatic herb. This sweet-and-sour, fragrant jelly is the result. You can vary the sharpness by altering the proportions of the lemons, limes and oranges. Different types of thyme will give different flavours.

Makes 4–6 jars per 1 litre
(1¼ pints or 4 cups) of juice

For the juice

1kg (2lb 4oz) unwaxed lemons, cut into quarters

1.5 litres (about 3 pints or 6⅓ cups) litres water

4 sprigs fresh thyme

For the jelly – for each
1 litre (1¼ pints or 4 cups)
of juice use

1kg (2lb 4oz or 5 cups) raw cane sugar

4 tbsp fresh thyme leaves, stripped off the stalks

1. Place the lemons in a large, heavy-bottomed preserving pan with the water and sprigs of thyme. Bring to the boil, cover, lower the heat and simmer for 1 hour, or until the fruit has turned really pulpy. Remove from the heat and pour into a jelly bag or doubled muslin suspended over a measuring jug or bowl. Leave long enough for the juice to completely drain through – generally over 3 hours but less than 24 hours.

2. Put a saucer in the fridge for the setting test. Measure the juice and weigh out an equal amount of sugar, then put both in a large, heavy-bottomed preserving pan and heat gently, stirring constantly, until the sugar has completely dissolved. Bring the mixture to the boil and boil until setting point has been reached – this should take about 10 minutes. The juice will change from opaque to clear as it gets close to setting point.

3. Remove the pan from the heat. To test for setting point drop a little of the jelly mixture onto the cold saucer, count to 10 and push it with your fingertip. If the jelly wrinkles, then setting point has been reached. If it doesn't wrinkle, return the pan to the heat, bring back to the boil and test again in a couple of minutes.

4. Once setting point has been reached, remove from the heat and leave for a minute before removing any scum on the surface. Add the thyme leaves and give a gentle but thorough stir. Stir very gently every 2 minutes while the jelly starts to cool to ensure the thyme is evenly distributed throughout and doesn't rise to the surface.

5. When the jelly has cooled down enough so that the jelly is still and the thyme leaves remain suspended in the jelly (about 5–10 minutes), pour into sterilised jars and put the lids on immediately. Separate the jars and leave to cool.

Mulled wine jelly

This rich jelly with its evocative spicing makes a delicious alternative to cranberry sauce with the Christmas turkey or goose. Our recipe uses redcurrants as the jelly base, but in the spirit of adventure, apples could be used instead.

*Makes 4–6 jars per 1 litre
(1¼ pints or 4 cups) of juice*

For the juice

1kg (2lb 4oz) redcurrants, stalks and all

1 litre (1¾ pints or 4 cups) water

For the mulled wine

225ml (8fl oz or 1 cup) red wine

100ml (3½fl oz or scant ½ cup) cider vinegar

30ml (2 tbsp) lemon juice

1.5g (½ tsp) ground nutmeg

½ tsp whole cloves

½ tsp (approximately 9) allspice berries

Pinch of ground cinnamon

*For the jelly – for each
1 litre (1¼ pints or 4 cups)
of juice use*

zest of half a medium orange

1kg (2lb 4oz or 5 cups) raw cane sugar

1. Rinse the redcurrants but don't bother taking them off the stalks; just put them in a pan with the water and bring to the boil. Lower the heat and simmer for 30 minutes until the fruit is soft and mushy. Remove from the heat and pour into a jelly bag or doubled muslin suspended over a measuring jug or bowl. Leave between 3 and 24 hours to let the juice strain through at its own gentle pace. Don't be tempted to squeeze the juice through as this will make the jelly cloudy.

2. Put a saucer in the fridge to test for setting point later on. To make the mulled wine put the red wine, vinegar, lemon juice and spices into a small pan and heat. Bring to just under a boil, lower the heat and simmer very gently for 10 minutes before removing from the heat. Strain through a sieve to remove the cloves and the allspice berries.

3. In a large, heavy-bottomed preserving pan, combine 1 litre (1¾ pints or 4 cups) of the redcurrant juice with the mulled wine, the orange zest and the sugar and bring to a rolling boil. Stir constantly until the sugar has dissolved. Bring the mixture to the boil and boil until the setting point is reached: this usually takes about 20 minutes.

4. Remove the pan from the heat and test for setting point by dropping a little of the jelly onto the cold saucer, count to 10 and push it with your fingertip. If the jelly wrinkles, then setting point has been reached. If setting point hasn't been reached, return the pan to the heat and continue boiling, testing every minute or two until the jelly crinkles on the surface.

5. Once the jelly has reached setting point, remove from the heat, skim off any scum on the surface and pour into sterilised jars. Put the lids on immediately. Separate the jars and leave to cool.

Apple, red pepper & chilli jelly

The West Indies are famous for their hot pepper jellies, and this versatile version has become a favourite in our office. Sweet, with a clear, vibrant heat that warms the taste buds instead of walloping them, it is good with everything from fish to cream cheese. Serve melted, it makes a piquant dipping sauce for fishcakes.

Makes 4–6 jars per 1 litre (1¼ pints or 4 cups) of juice

For the juice

1kg (2lb 4oz) or approximately 4 large Bramley apples, roughly chopped

1 litre (1¾ pints or 4 cups) water

For the jelly –
for each 1 litre (1¼ pints or 4 cups) of juice use

1kg (2lb 4oz or 5 cups) raw cane sugar

25ml (1fl oz or 1 tbsp + 2 tsp) lemon juice

½ diced red pepper, deseeded and finely chopped

1 fresh red chilli, deseeded and finely chopped

1. Put the apple pieces in a large, heavy-bottomed preserving pan. Cover with the water. Bring to the boil, lower the heat and simmer for 20 minutes, or until the apples are soft and mushy. Remove from the heat and pour into a jelly bag or doubled muslin suspended over a measuring jug or bowl. Leave between 3 and 24 hours to let the juice strain through at its own gentle pace. Remember not to squeeze the muslin as this will turn your jelly cloudy.

2. Put a saucer in the fridge for the setting test. Measure the beautiful pale-pink apple juice and put into a large, heavy-bottomed preserving pan with an equal amount of sugar. Heat gently, stirring constantly until the sugar has completely dissolved, then bring to a rolling boil. Add the lemon juice and bring back to a vigorous boil, stirring occasionally until the mixture reaches setting point – this should take about 20 minutes.

3. To test for setting point, remove the pan from the heat and drop a little of the jelly mixture onto the cold saucer, count to 10 and push the jelly with your fingertip. If the jelly wrinkles, then setting point has been reached. If it doesn't wrinkle, return the pan to the heat and continue boiling, testing every minute or two until the jelly wrinkles on the saucer.

4. Once setting point has been reached, remove from the heat. Skim off any scum that has risen to the surface, using a small sieve or slotted spoon, and stir in the pepper and chilli. Stir very gently every 2 minutes while the jelly starts to cool to ensure that the pepper and chilli are evenly distributed throughout and don't float to the surface.

5. When the jelly has cooled enough so that it's still liquid but the pepper and chilli pieces have stopped rising (about 5–10 minutes), pour it into sterilised jars and seal immediately. Separate the jars and leave to cool.

Apple & mint jelly

Best known for the wonderful way it complements lamb and livens up new potatoes, soft-set mint jelly is a store-cupboard essential. We use mild-flavoured spearmint, but there are many different varieties and all bring their own distinct characteristic to a homemade jelly. Best grown in pots because of its over-enthusiastic tendency to go on the rampage, mint will have its best flavour in early summer before flowering. For jelly-making pick soft, young leaves.

*Makes 4–6 jars per 1 litre
(1¼ pints or 4 cups) of juice*

For the juice

1kg (2lb 4oz) or approximately 4 large Bramley apples, roughly chopped into quarters

1 litre (1¾ pints or 4 cups) water

*For the jelly –
for each 1 litre (1¼ pints or 4 cups)
of juice use*

1kg (2lb 4oz or 5 cups) raw cane sugar

25ml (1fl oz or 1 tbsp + 2 tsp) lemon juice

a large handful of fresh mint leaves, washed and finely chopped

1. Put the apple quarters in a large, heavy-bottomed preserving pan and cover with the water. Bring to the boil, lower the heat and simmer for 20 minutes, or until the apples are soft and mushy. Remove from the heat and pour into a jelly bag or doubled muslin suspended over a measuring jug or bowl. Leave between 3 hours or overnight (but no longer than 24 hours) to let the juice strain through at its own gentle pace. Don't be tempted to squeeze the juice through the muslin or your jelly will end up cloudy.

2. You should have about 1 litre (1¾ pints or 4 cups) of pale-pink juice scenting your kitchen. Put a saucer in the fridge to cool for the setting test. Measure the juice and put into the preserving pan with an equal amount of sugar. Heat gently and stir until the sugar has completely dissolved, then add the lemon juice and bring to a rolling boil. Boil until the mixture reaches setting point – this should take about 20 minutes – stirring regularly.

3. To test for setting point, put a drop of the jelly mixture onto the cold saucer, count to 10 and push the jelly with your fingertip. If the jelly wrinkles, then setting point has been reached. If it doesn't wrinkle, return the pan to the heat and continue boiling, testing every minute or two until the jelly crinkles on the saucer.

4. Once setting point has been reached, remove from the heat. Skim off any scum that has risen to the surface, then stir in the mint. Stir very gently every couple of minutes while the jelly starts to cool to ensure that the mint is evenly distributed throughout and doesn't float to the surface.

5. When the jelly has cooled down enough so that it's still liquid but the mint has stopped rising (about 5–10 minutes), pour into sterilised jars and put on the lids immediately. Separate the jars and leave to cool.

Apple & sage jelly

Living in Wiltshire which is famous for its pigs, we have to include this delicious accompaniment to roast pork, both hot or cold. Just the thought of smothering the tender meat with this soft-set, fragrant jelly is enough to get our salivary glands going crazy. Sage can be picked throughout the year, but has its best flavour in spring and early summer. Pick on a warm, dry day.

Makes 4–6 jars per 1 litre (1¼ pints or 4 cups) of juice

For the juice

1kg (2lb 4oz) or approximately 4 large Bramley apples, roughly chopped into quarters

1 litre (1¾ pints or 4 cups) water

For the jelly –
for each 1 litre (1¼ pints or 4 cups) of juice use

1kg (2lb 4oz or 5 cups) raw cane sugar

25ml (1fl oz or 1 tbsp + 2 tsp) lemon juice

a large handful of fresh sage leaves, washed and very finely chopped

1. Put the apples in a large, heavy-bottomed preserving pan. Cover with the water, bring to the boil, lower the heat and simmer for 20 minutes until the apples are soft and pulpy. Remove from the heat and pour the juice into a jelly bag or doubled muslin suspended over a measuring jug or bowl. Leave between 3 hours and overnight (but no longer than 24 hours) to let the juice strain through gently. Don't be tempted to squeeze the the muslin as this will make your jelly cloudy.

2. When the juice has run through, you should have about 1 litre (1¾ pints or 4 cups) of pale-pink apple nectar perfuming your home. Put a saucer in the fridge for the setting test. Put the juice and an equal weight of sugar in a large, heavy-bottomed preserving pan. Heat gently and stir until the sugar has completely dissolved, then add the lemon juice and bring to a rolling boil. Boil until the mixture reaches setting point – this should take about 20 minutes – stirring regularly.

3. Remove the pan from the heat and test for setting point by dropping a little of the jelly onto the cold saucer, count to 10 and push it with your fingertip. If the jelly wrinkles, then setting point has been reached. If setting point hasn't been reached, return the pan to the heat and continue boiling, testing every minute or two until the jelly wrinkles on the surface.

4. Once setting point has been reached, remove the pan from the heat. Skim off any scum that has risen to the surface and stir in the sage. Stir very gently every couple of minutes while the jelly starts to cool to ensure that the sage is evenly distributed throughout.

5. When the jelly has cooled down enough so that it's still liquid but the flecks of sage have stopped rising (about 5–10 minutes), pour into sterilised jars and put the lids on immediately. Separate the jars and leave to cool.

Rosemary jelly

We exhibit at around 20 food shows a year, from county fairs to large exhibition halls, and we always open a jar of our rosemary jelly for people to taste. Without fail its sweet, herby flavour delights everyone who tries it. We use very young, tender rosemary leaves chopped up and suspended in the clear jelly, but if your rosemary is a bit older and woodier, you may want to suspend just a sprig of rosemary in each jar.

Makes 4–6 jars per 1 litre
(1¼ pints or 4 cups) of juice

For the juice

1kg (2lb 4oz) or approximately 4 large Bramley apples, roughly chopped

5 sprigs of rosemary

1 litre (1¾ pints or 4 cups) water

For the jelly –
for each 1 litre (1¼ pints or 4 cups)
of juice use

1kg (2lb 4oz or 5 cups) raw cane sugar

30ml (1fl oz or 2 tbsp) lemon juice

Either 20g (¾oz) fresh rosemary leaves, finely chopped, or whole sprigs, one for each jar

1. Put the apples and rosemary in a large, heavy-bottomed preserving pan and cover with the water. Bring to the boil, cover, lower the heat and simmer for about 20 minutes, or until the apples are soft and pulpy. Remove from the heat and pour through a jelly bag or doubled muslin suspended over a measuring jug or bowl. Leave between 3 hours and overnight (but no longer than 24 hours) to allow the juice to drain gently through. Don't be tempted to squeeze the muslin or this will make your jelly cloudy.

2. Put a saucer in the fridge for the setting-point test later on. Measure out an equal amount of sugar to apple juice and put both in a large, heavy-bottomed preserving pan. Heat slowly and stir continually until all the sugar has completely dissolved, then quickly bring to a vigorous, rolling boil. Add the lemon juice and bring back to the boil. Boil until the liquid reaches setting point: this should take about 20 minutes.

3. To test for setting point, put a drop of the jelly mixture onto the cold saucer, count to 10 and push the jelly with your fingertip. If the jelly wrinkles, then setting point has been reached. If it doesn't wrinkle, return the pan to the heat and continue boiling, testing every minute or two.

4. If using chopped rosemary, once the setting point is reached, remove the pan from the heat and add the rosemary, stirring gently. Keep stirring gently every 5 minutes while the jelly cools to ensure that the pieces of herb are evenly distributed through the jelly and don't rise to the surface.

5. Once the jelly has cooled enough so that the rosemary has stopped rising (about 5–10 minutes), pour into sterilised jars and put the lids on immediately. Alternatively, when setting point is reached, pour into the jars, leave for 15 minutes, then push a sprig of rosemary into each jar before putting on the lids. Separate the jars and leave to cool.

Rowan jelly

This authentic hedgerow jelly uses the vibrant red berries of the mountain ash tree, which appear in early autumn, alongside the trusty crab apple. Although packed with vitamins A and C, rowan berries can be slightly dry, which is why they are so readily paired with tart, juicy crab apples. The beautiful red jelly has a faintly smoky aroma, which makes it an ideal accompaniment for venison. In her book *Food in England*, Dorothy Hartley recommends eating it '…with mountain meats, just as you would serve redcurrant jelly with valley meat'.

Makes 4–6 jars per 1 litre
(1¼ pints or 4 cups) of juice

For the juice

500g (1lb 2oz) rowan berries, washed and removed from their stalks

500g (1lb 2oz) crab apples, roughly chopped

Water to cover

For the jelly –
for each 1 litre (1¼ pints or 4 cups)
of juice use

1kg (2lb 4oz or 5 cups) raw cane sugar

30ml (1fl oz or 2 tbsp) lemon juice

1. Put the rowan berries and crab apples in a large, heavy-bottomed preserving pan filled with just enough water to cover.

2. Bring to the boil, cover, lower the heat and simmer for about 20–30 minutes, or until the fruit is soft and pulpy. Remove from the heat and pour through a jelly bag or doubled muslin suspended over a measuring jug or bowl. Leave between 3 hours and overnight (but no longer than 24 hours) to allow the juice to drain gently through. Remember not to squeeze the juice through the muslin or this will make your jelly cloudy.

3. Put a saucer in the fridge for the setting-point test later on. Measure out an equal amount of sugar to juice and put both in a large, heavy-bottomed preserving pan. Heat slowly and stir continually until all the sugar has completely dissolved, then quickly bring to a vigorous, rolling boil. Add the lemon juice and bring back to the boil. Boil until the liquid reaches setting point: this should take about 20 minutes.

4. To test for setting point, put a drop of the jelly mixture onto the cold saucer, count to 10 and push the jelly with your fingertip. If the jelly wrinkles, then setting point has been reached. If it doesn't wrinkle, return the pan to the heat and continue boiling, testing every minute or two.

5. Once setting point has been reached, remove the pan from the heat, skim off any scum on the surface and pour into sterilised jars. Put the lids on immediately. Separate the jars and leave to cool.

Quince cheese

Tip

If you want to serve the cheese in slices make it in straight-sided jars so the cheese will turn out easily.

One fine, sunny Sunday evening in September, our MD, Guy, was driving the company van home after spending the weekend working at a food fair. Concentrating on navigating his way slowly through a small, sleepy village and singing away to some tunes, he was startled when there was a bang on the side of the van and a girl's face appeared at the passenger window. 'Hello, Tracklements! Would you like to buy some quinces?'

The quinces in question were on 30 trees that had been planted to help fill out an apple orchard; consequently the fruit had no home and would have been wasted. Keen to avoid the wastage, Guy said yes, and that's why every September we welcome the delivery of these fruits with their incredible, heady scent. We leave them for a couple of days to develop a 'bloom' on their skins, and by the time we're ready to use them the whole factory smells good enough to eat.

Fruit cheeses go particularly well with a selection of hard cheeses, particularly salty, nutty or sour ones.

Makes 6 ramekins or straight-sided small jars

1kg (2lb 4oz) quinces, washed and chopped into smallish pieces

500ml (18fl oz or 2¼ cups) water

1kg (2lb 4oz or 5 cups) raw cane sugar per 1kg (2lb 4oz) fruit purée

1. Put the quince pieces into a large, heavy-bottomed preserving pan. Pour over just enough water to cover and bring to a gentle boil. Lower the heat and simmer for about 30 minutes until the fruit is soft and pulpy.

2. Remove from the heat and rub through a sieve into a bowl using the back of a wooden spoon. Alternatively, put the fruity mash through a mouli on a fine setting.

3. Weigh the fruit purée and put it into a large, heavy-bottomed preserving pan, adding an equal weight of sugar. Heat gently and stir continuously until the sugar has dissolved, then quickly bring to a rolling boil. Boil for about 20 minutes, or until the mixture is thick enough so that when you draw the spoon across the bottom of the pan, the resultant channel doesn't fill immediately.

4. Pour into sterilised ramekins or jars and cover with clingfilm or seal the jars immediately. The cheese will keep for up to two years if put in an airtight jar.

Damson cheese

This recipe for damson cheese is borrowed from my mother, who, every September, won herself an afternoon of peace and quiet by sending us out armed with ladders and buckets to find and collect the damsons that lined the local hedgerows. Only once was there a mishap when a ladder slipped, leaving my sister hanging from the tree; unfortunately we were giggling too much to be helpful and so she fell to the earth with a bump! We ate the resulting rich and fruity concoction with everything.

Makes 6 ramekins or straight-sided small jars

3kg (6½lb) damsons, washed

500ml (18fl oz or 2¼ cups) water

1kg (2lb 4oz or 5 cups) raw cane sugar per 1kg (2lb 4oz) fruit purée

1. Put the whole fruit in a large, heavy-bottomed preserving pan. For each 3kg (6½lb) of fruit, add 500ml (18fl oz or 2¼ cups) water and bring to the boil. Lower the heat and simmer for about 30 minutes until the fruit is soft and has disintegrated.

2. Remove the pan from the heat and allow the fruit to cool. Press the fruit through a sieve into a bowl using the back of a wooden spoon to remove the stones, or remove the stones first, then purée the fruit in a food processor. Alternatively, you can use a mouli on a fine setting. Pressing through a sieve is harder work, but like most things that are done by hand, it pays dividends as it ensures that the final cheese doesn't contain pieces of skin or stone.

3. Weigh the fruit purée and put it into a large, heavy-bottomed preserving pan, adding an equal weight of sugar. Heat gently and stir continuously until the sugar has dissolved, then quickly bring to a rolling boil. Boil for about 20 minutes, or until the mixture is thick enough so that when you draw the spoon across the bottom of the pan, the resultant channel doesn't fill immediately.

4. Pour the mixture into sterilised ramekins or jars and cover with clingfilm or seal immediately. The cheese will keep for up to two years if put in an airtight jar.

Tip

If you want to serve the cheese in slices make it in straight-sided jars so the cheese will turn out easily.

Gooseberry cheese

Making this fruit cheese is like pure alchemy: you take a sour, hard, green fruit and, using only water, lemon and sugar, transform it into a rosy-coloured, velvet-textured, sweet delight, dripping in English summeriness. You can almost hear the bees buzzing and smell the freshly cut grass. It can be made using the leftover pulp from Gooseberry & Elderflower Jelly (see page 163), but if you have enough gooseberries, it's lovely to add some whole ones to pep up the fruitiness of the cheese.

Makes 6 ramekins or straight-sided small jars

1kg (2lb 4oz) whole gooseberrries

500ml (18fl oz or 2¼ cups) water

1kg (2lb 4oz or 5 cups) raw cane sugar per 1kg (2lb 4oz) fruit purée

Juice of ½ a lemon

1. Put the gooseberries (no need to top and tail) in a heavy-bottomed pan with the water, just enough to cover them. Bring to the boil, lower the heat and simmer for 20–30 minutes until the fruit has burst and lost its shape.

2. Pour the hot gooseberry mixture into a sieve over a bowl and press the purée through the sieve with a spatula or the back of a wooden spoon. Alternatively, you can use a mouli on a fine setting. Weigh the purée and put it into a large, heavy-bottomed preserving pan, adding an equal weight of sugar.

3. Heat gently and stir continuously until the sugar has dissolved. Then add the lemon juice and boil for 30–40 minutes until the mixture is like molten lava; it might bubble and spit. Stir regularly to stop it from sticking to the bottom of the pan. Boil until the mixture is thick enough so that when you draw the spoon across the bottom of the pan, the resultant channel doesn't fill immediately.

4. Pour the mixture into sterilised ramekins or jars and cover with clingfilm or seal immediately. The cheese will keep for up to two years if put in an airtight jar.

Tip

If you want to serve the cheese in slices make it in straight-sided jars so the cheese will turn out easily.

Tomato jam

Technically more of a 'cheese' than a jam, this set preserve has a very delicate flavour that is lovely when spread on cream cheese on a cracker, or served with a good, salty cheese. Achieving a solid set can be a bit of a challenge because tomatoes don't have much natural pectin, so we recommend starting the cooking process as quickly as possible after quartering the tomatoes to prevent what little pectin they have from dissipating.

We buy most of our tomatoes from the Isle of Wight, where there is more sunshine than on the UK mainland, and so the tomatoes are really luscious and ripe.

Makes 3–4 small jars

1kg (2lb 4oz) tomatoes, quartered

½ cinnamon stick

3 whole cloves

3 allspice berries

Zest of 1 lemon

1kg (2lb 4oz or 5 cups) raw cane sugar per 1kg (2lb 4oz) fruit purée

15ml (½fl oz or 1 tbsp) lemon juice

1. Place the tomotoes in a large, heavy-bottomed preserving pan with the cinnamon, cloves, allspice berries and lemon zest. Quickly bring to the boil, then lower the heat and simmer for 15 minutes.

2. Remove from the heat. Discard the cinnamon stick. Pour the hot tomato mixture into a sieve set over a bowl and press the purée through the sieve with a spatula or the back of a wooden spoon, checking that all the spices have been removed. Alternatively, you can use a mouli on a fine setting.

3. Weigh the tomato purée and put in a large, heavy-bottomed preserving pan. Add an equal amount of sugar and the lemon juice. Heat gently until the sugar has dissolved, stirring constantly. Bring to a rolling boil, still stirring constantly – be careful as the bubbling tomato mixture will spit. Boil for about 20 minutes, or until the mixture is thick enough so that when you draw the spoon across the bottom of the pan, the resultant channel doesn't fill immediately.

4. Pour into sterilised jars and put the lids on immediately. The jam will keep for six months.

Apple butter

Like a cheese but with a softer set, fruit butters are smooth and
luscious and happily cross the divide between savoury and sweet,
accompanying pork as well as pancakes. Our MD, Guy, has longed to
make a Tracklements apple butter, and is frequently found scouring
old cookbooks in search of the perfect recipe. We think this one, which
is a take on Herbert Mace's 1940s' version, is pretty much there.

Makes 3–5 small jars
1 litre (2 pints or 4 cups) dry cider
500g (1lb 2oz) or 2
Bramley apples
500g (1lb 2oz) or 3 eating apples
Zest and juice of 1 lemon
1 tsp ground cinnamon
400g (14oz or 2 cups)
raw cane sugar

1. Pour the cider into a large, heavy-bottomed pan and bring to a vigorous
boil until reduced by half. While it boils, chop the apples roughly – cores,
skin and all.

2. Once the cider has reduced, add the apples, lemon zest and juice
and simmer until the apples are completely soft – this should take about
20 minutes.

3. Remove the pan from the heat and allow to cool for a couple of minutes
before pouring the fruity mash into a sieve over a bowl. Press the apple
mixture through the sieve with a spatula or the back of a wooden spoon.
Alternatively, put the mash through a mouli on a fine setting.

4. Put the apple purée into a clean, large, heavy-bottomed preserving
pan, along with the cinnamon and sugar and heat gently until the sugar
has dissolved. Bring to the boil, stirring regularly, until the mixture has
thickened to the desired consistency, so that when you draw the spoon across
the bottom of the pan, the resultant channel doesn't fill immediately.

5. Pour into sterilised jars and put the lids on immediately. The butter will
keep for six months.

Variation

To make a spicier variation, Apple
and Chilli Butter, leave out the
cinnamon and add 1 fresh red
chilli (deseeded and very, very
finely chopped) with the sugar at
the beginning of step 4.

Pear butter

A strong early autumn wind can strip pears from their branches before they are ready to eat and these windfalls, although not as soft and yielding as their ripe counterparts, are perfect for the home preserver. Pear Butter is sweet and luxurious and makes a really good alternative filling for a Victoria sponge cake or for spreading on malt loaf.

Makes 3–5 small jars

1kg (2lb 4oz or 5) pears, quartered

400ml (14fl oz or 1¾ cups) water

½ tsp ground allspice

½ tsp ground cloves

400g (14oz or 2 cups) raw cane sugar

1. Place the pears in a large, heavy-bottomed pan, along with the water. Bring to the boil, lower the heat and simmer for about 30 minutes until the fruit is soft.

2. Remove the pan from the heat and allow to cool for a couple of minutes before pouring the fruity mash into a sieve over a pan. Press the pear mixture through the sieve with a spatula or the back of a wooden spoon. Alternatively, you can use a mouli on a fine setting.

3. Put the fruit purée into a clean pan, add the ground spices and sugar and heat gently until all the sugar has dissolved. Bring to the boil, stirring regularly until the mixture has thickened to the desired consistency, so that when you draw the spoon across the bottom of the pan, the resultant channel doesn't fill immediately.

4. Pour into sterilised jars and put on the lids immediately. The butter will keep for six months.

The last spoonful...

Even the most ardent of condiment-lovers will, on some occasions, find a random jar tucked away in the back of the cupboard, or hiding behind the butter in the fridge looking lost, unloved and uninspiring with just a spoonful or scraping of contents left in the jar. Sometimes we get stuck for ideas and think a chutney is only suitable for the cheeseboard, a pickle is only good with a ploughman's lunch and a relish with a sandwich – but historically there was no division between savoury and sweet; frequently, if you think of a preserve as a delicious concentration of flavours you will find inspiration for different ways to use them.

If you hate waste, don't throw out this last morsel of goodness, so here are some suggestions as to what to do with 'the last spoonful'.

- Change the way it looks – turn chutneys, pickles and sauces into a flavour-boosting stock cube by whizzing with a stick blender or mashing with a fork.
- Turn it into a dip – add it to sour cream, cream cheese or yogurt. Use a squeeze of lemon or lime juice to bring the flavours together.
- Use with potato or rice salads – mix with a little mayo to make a fantastically different sauce.
- Use with pasta or couscous – stir in a spoonful to make a sauce.
- Make a marinade – melted jellies and mustards mixed together with a little oil make great-tasting marinades for meat.
- Jellies are great for deglazing your frying pan and adding to the meat juices to make a sauce for meat.
- Salad dressings and vinaigrettes are best for leftover mustard: try mixing into an olive oil/vinegar combo; three parts oil to one part vinegar. What's the worst that can happen?
- Gravy, sauces or casseroles – a spoonful of leftover preserve in any of these will add extra oomph.
- Mustard mash – add leftover mustard to mashed potato, carrot or swede instead of freshly ground black pepper to give it a boost.
- Stir-fries – anything fruity and sweet goes well in a stir-fry.
- Eggs – whether you're making an omelette or scrambled eggs, a couple of teaspoons of leftover chutney, mustard or sauce in the mix will go down a treat.

- Scones, muffins and cheese biscuits – add a spoonful of chutneys, mustards and jellies to the dough before cooking.
- Add a spoonful to minced meat when making meatballs or burgers to give the meat a lift.
- Jellies work well warmed, and spooned over soft, creamy cheese.
- Make a delicious sauce for crêpes or ice cream – add a spoonful of brandy, sherry or a liqueur to a warmed jelly or fruit sauce.

Index

Acknowledgements

This edition published in the
United Kingdom in 2019 by
Pavilion
43 Great Ormond Street
London WC1N 3HZ

First edition published in 2014

ISBN: 978-1-911624-68-4

10 9 8 7 6 5 4 3 2 1

A CIP catalogue record for this book
is available from the British Library

Repro by Rival Colour Ltd, UK
Printed by 1010 Printing
International Ltd, China

www.pavilionbooks.com

Additional photographs
Alamy page 15 (Tim Hill); page 70
(Funkyfood London/Paul Williams);
page 136 (William Mullins); page 183
(Fabrizio Troiani); GAP Photos
page 42 (Tommy Tonsberg)

Thanks to all our stalwart supporters, people who have volunteered their
recipes and everyone at Tracklements who are dedicated to the principles
of making good food. Thanks also to the insatiable appetite of our founder
William Tullberg whose curiosity resulted in the creation of a truly
exceptional business, also his wife Jennifer who helped to get Tracklements
out of his kitchen and into yours.

Thanks are also due to Alex Evelyn for paving the way for this book with
her excellent, informative and entertaining blog of Tracklements recipes.
Fran Warde for her invaluable advice and everyone who has helped to make
this book possible.

We also want to thank Becca Spry and Fiona Holman of Pavilion Books
and our editor Jamie Ambrose for showing us the ropes and believing in
this book. Many thanks must also go to Izzy Holton for this updated edition.

But mainly I want to thank everyone who makes good food, eats good
food and shares good food; particularly those who have shared it with me!